God the Geometer

God the Geometer

How Science Supports Faith

THOMAS J. McAVOY

RESOURCE *Publications* · Eugene, Oregon

GOD THE GEOMETER
How Science Supports Faith

Copyright © 2024 Thomas J. McAvoy. All rights reserved. Except for brief quotations in critical publications or reviews, no part of this book may be reproduced in any manner without prior written permission from the publisher. Write: Permissions, Wipf and Stock Publishers, 199 W. 8th Ave., Suite 3, Eugene, OR 97401.

Resource Publications
An Imprint of Wipf and Stock Publishers
199 W. 8th Ave., Suite 3
Eugene, OR 97401

www.wipfandstock.com

PAPERBACK ISBN: 979-8-3852-0827-2
HARDCOVER ISBN: 979-8-3852-0828-9
EBOOK ISBN: 979-8-3852-0829-6

VERSION NUMBER 02/13/24

Scripture taken from New Century Version (NCV), Copyright © 2005 by Thomas Nelson, Used by permission, All rights reserved, Thomas Nelson, Inc., Nashville, TN.

Specialized finch beaks noted by Darwin, reproduced with permission from John van Wyhe ed. 2002, The Complete Work of Charles Darwin Online.

Reverend O'Conner's detailed report on John Traynor's cure, entitled: I Met A Miracle, was originally published by St. Columban's Foreign Mission Society in 1944. It is used with permission of the Mission Society of St. Columban and the Catholic Truth Society which published Reverend O'Conner's report in 1965.

Photos of the Shroud of Turin from Vern Miller collection, © Vernon Miller, 1978. Permission to use images given by copyright holder, D'Muhala and Lavoie Trust, 2018.

The description of Our Lady of Guadalupe in chapter 11 is taken from a writeup on the Knights of Columbus website (www.kofc.org) and it is reprinted with their permission.

The description of Modern Eucharistic Miracles in chapter 11 is taken from an article published by Jeanette Williams available at AscensionPress.com. Reprinted with the permission of Ascension Press.

To
Jessie and Susan
Both of whom inspired and supported me

Contents

List of Illustrations and Tables | ix
Acknowledgements | xi

1. Introduction and Goal of Book | 1
2. The Big Bang | 12
3. Fine-Tuning in the Universe | 26
4. Fine-Tuning in Our Solar System | 35
5. Would a Rerun of Evolution Lead to Intelligent Life? | 47
6. What Is the Purpose of Evolution? | 56
7. Why Intelligent Design Is Not Valid Science | 68
8. Free Will and Quantum Indeterminacy | 77
9. Freedom and Natural Evil | 87
10. Healing Miracles | 95
11. Physical Miracles | 106
12. Conclusions | 121

Appendix A: Electromagnetic Force and Radiation | 129
Appendix B: Proteins | 134
Appendix C: Genetic Algorithms | 137
Glossary | 143
Bibliography | 153
Index | 159

List of Illustrations and Tables

Figure 2.1. Expansion of universe after the Big Bang | 13

Figure 2.2. Hubble's distance-velocity plot for stars | 15

Figure 2.3. Schematic diagram of deuterium atom | 16

Figure 2.4. Fusion of hydrogen isotopes to helium DOE | 18

Figure 2.5. CBOE data and black body spectrum | 21

Figure 2.6. Nagasaki after the atomic bomb explosion | 24

Figure 3.1. Schematic diagram of helium atom | 27

Figure 4.1. Our Solar System. A relative size of planets. B Distance from Sun from Wikipedia | 36

Figure 4.2. Almost circular solar system orbit in a spiral galaxy. ESA/Hubble | 37

Table 4.1 Star types and properties (°C = °K −273) | 39

Figure 4.3. Tidally locked planet orbiting a red dwarf | 40

Figure 4.4. Continental drift in Iceland | 41

Figure 4.5. Illustration of Earth's axis of rotation | 43

Figure 4.6. Change in Earth's Axis of Rotation without a Moon over Time | 44

Figure 5.1. Double Helix Structure of DNA | 50

Figure 6.1. Topographical map showing peaks | 59

Figure 6.2. Specialized finch beaks noted by Darwin | 60

List of Illustrations and Tables

Figure 7.1. Mouse trap | 71

Figure 8.1. Double slit experimental setup | 79

Figure 10.1. Jack Traynor the invalid leaving for Lourdes, July 21, 1923, Lime Street Station, Liverpool | 101

Figure 10.2. Jack Traynor arriving home from Lourdes | 103

Figure 11.1. Positive(a) and Negative(b) Images of Shroud of Turin and Blow Up of Hand Area(c) | 107

Figure 11.2 Professor Fanti with Holy Fire in 2019 | 111

Figure 11.3. Juan Diego's Original Tilma | 114

Figure 11.4. Crowd Watching the Miracle of the Sun October 13, 1917 | 120

Figure A-1. Earth's magnetic field | 130

Figure A-2. Electromagnetic spectrum | 132

Figure B-1. Chemical structure of glycine | 135

Figure B-2. Chemical structure of alanine | 135

Figure B-3. Peptide bond between glycine and alanine | 136

Figure C-1. Topographical map showing peaks | 138

Acknowledgements

I WANT TO ACKNOWLEDGE both Jessie and Susan for the inspiration and support they provided to me for writing this book. Jessie was my first wife for just shy of forty-two years. She tragically passed away much too early from a rare and debilitating cancer. Her courage in struggling with her disease was inspirational for me and my three children. While she was struggling and after her passing I began to question why such a miserable disease exits in our world. To get answers I started a decades-long study of science and the Bible. This book is the result of that effort.

After Jessie's passing I was reintroduced to my current wife Susan. She had lost her husband, Lou, to a rare disease as well. Thus, Susan also appreciates how life can seem unfair at times and her experiences have helped strengthen her faith. Through Susan's influence and inspiration, I became more devoted to my religion and both of us try to attend daily Mass. Susan and I have been married for almost seventeen years and she has strongly supported and encouraged me in writing this book. Susan and Lou also had three children, and I have been blessed to become grandpa to their nine children. I also have five grandchildren of my own, and one great grandchild. One of my primary motivations in writing this book is to convey the insights I have learned over the years about how science supports faith to all Susan's and my children and grandchildren.

I also want to acknowledge Father Joseph Quigley who was chaplain at the Newman Center at the University of Massachusetts (UMASS) when I taught there. Father Joe was a great friend who had a very practical approach to faith. His motto was: "Do the best you can and leave the rest up to the Lord." He greatly impacted my life and the lives of all the students he counseled and shepherded over the years. He fondly called them his sons

Acknowledgements

and daughters. I learned a great deal from Father Joe about faith and how it should be practiced.

At UMASS I had a terrific department chair, John Eldridge, from whom I learned a great deal. At the University of Maryland, where I also taught, Jan Sengers was my department chair and he was not only a strong leader but very helpful in suggesting potential endorsers for this book. I want to express my thanks to Dr. Janice Hicks, Joe Marino, Dr. Gil Lavoie, and Prof. Cees Dekker for taking the time to read my manuscript, for providing helpful feedback and endorsements for this book. I also want to acknowledge Father Paul Caron and Father Chris Stanibula for inviting me to give talks on faith and science at St. Anthony's Parish in Mattapoisett, Massachusetts.

I also want to acknowledge my parents, Theresa and Thomas, who brought me up within the Catholic faith and were devoted to it. In addition, I acknowledge the teachers who educated me over the years. I was fortunate to have attended both a Catholic grammar school run by the Sisters of St. Joseph, and a Catholic high school run by the Jesuits. Over the years I myself have had many wonderful students that I had had the opportunity to interact with and learn from.

1

Introduction and Goal of Book

IN WRITING THIS BOOK on how science supports faith I discovered the image of God the Geometer shown on the cover of the book. The image appeared in the Codex Vindobonensis 2554, a famous manuscript dated to 1220–230. The description given with the image on Wikipedia is as follows:

> *Science*, and particularly *geometry* and *astronomy/astrology*, was linked directly to the divine for most medieval scholars. The compass in this 13th century manuscript is a symbol of God's act of *Creation*. God has created the universe after geometric and harmonic principles, to seek these principles was therefore to seek and worship God.[1]

My goal in writing this book is to demonstrate the validity of the last sentence in this description by showing how modern science, particularly cosmology, physics, astronomy, and evolution, provides strong support for faith in God and how science is not in conflict with such faith.

In 1834 William Whewell who was a master at Trinity College in Cambridge coined the phrase "scientist."[2] Prior to 1834 scientists were referred to as natural philosophers. It is not clear when the word "science," which comes from the Latin, *scientia*, was coined. Science deals with the

---

1. "God," Description.
2. Lewis, *Heat and Thermodynamics*, 95.

physical world and it makes hypotheses that can be tested and whose truth can thereby be determined.

Since medieval times human knowledge of science has grown enormously, particularly in the last century. The advances made by science over the last century or so have been truly remarkable. Consider the advances in aviation. The Wright brothers flight of the first aircraft took place in 1903. Today people jet all over the globe at speeds that would have been unimaginable in 1903. Consider the advances in communications. Alexander Graham Bell received a patent on the telephone in 1876. Today most people have cell phones and they use them just about everywhere not only for communicating but also for looking up information on the web. Cell phones are also great for getting driving directions, including optimizing routes due to traffic delays. The world wide web dates from 1989 and it has changed life all over the globe. One can find just about anything on the web from restaurant locations and menus to historical information to sports scores, etc.

What humans have learned about the origin and development of our universe, the study of cosmology, has been truly remarkable. Today the overwhelming majority of cosmologists believe that our universe started roughly 13.8 billion years ago, with what has been labeled the Big Bang. Cosmologists have been able to: (1) calculate what happened fractions of a second after the Big Bang; (2) to determine the history of star formation in the universe and its relationship to the formation of the atomic species necessary for life to exist; and (3) to verify the Big Bang hypothesis by measuring the microwave background radiation[3] which was produced by the Big Bang. It is truly amazing what has been learned about the very ancient history of our universe.

Over the last century there have been remarkable advances in chemistry which resulted in major benefits to mankind. The materials that are available today would amaze someone living one hundred years ago. Included would be plastics such as Teflon and smart materials that change their properties when exposed to temperature, moisture, or electric fields. We are beginning to apply biology to the benefit of how people live. James Watson and Francis Crick discovered the double helix structure of DNA in 1953. The human genome has been sequenced in 2003 and today genetic information is being used routinely to improve medicine. These are just a few examples of how science has affected people's lives.

3. Microwave radiation is explained in Appendix A.

Introduction and Goal of Book

The average person is in awe of the accomplishments of science; the average person is also overwhelmed by the complexity of science today. Indeed, professional scientists and engineers are also overwhelmed by this complexity. I have a Ph.D. in chemical engineering, which I taught for just under forty years at two universities. I currently have an emeritus faculty appointment in the Department of Chemical and Biomolecular Engineering at the University of Maryland. Yet, I am constantly amazed and overwhelmed by what science and engineering are accomplishing today. The advances are truly breathtaking.

The English word "faith" is thought to date from 1200 to 1250. The word faith is derived from Latin, *fides*, and old French, *feid*,[4] and it connotes confidence or trust in a person, thing, or concept. In this text faith refers to trust in God. Although the word faith is medieval, the concept of faith is discussed in both the Old and New Testaments. In the Gospels faith appears over three hundred times. For example, "whatever you ask in prayer, you will receive, if you have faith" (Matt 21:22).

Faith today is not as strong as it was one hundred years ago. Advances made by mankind can lead people to think that faith is passé, and no longer necessary. More recently, I believe church scandals with pedophilia led to a downturn in church attendance. The scandals contributed to creating a vacuum in terms of spirituality, resulting in people discounting what the church taught. I believe this vacuum was filled by the "woke" movement which is a type of pseudo-religion. This movement is not only fervent but it also espouses many anti-religious ideas, e.g. abortion right up to the time of birth. Anyone who speaks out against this movement is cancelled in a manner reminiscent of the medieval inquisition.

The initial conflict between faith as represented by the Catholic Church and science can be traced to Copernicus (1473–1543), who was a Polish astronomer. Sometime between 1508 and 1514 Copernicus wrote about his theory that the Earth revolved around the Sun, i.e. his heliocentric theory. This theory disagreed with church teaching at the time based on Scripture that stated that the Earth was the center of the universe. Galileo (1564–1642) using a better telescope than Copernicus confirmed his heliocentric theory and he published a book on his results in 1610. In 1633 Galileo was tried for heresy by the Roman Catholic inquisition. He was sentenced to house arrest until his death.

---

4. "Faith," para. 2.

God the Geometer

The most important conflict between faith and science no doubt resulted from Darwin's book, *On the Origin of Species*,[5] published in 1859. In it, Darwin proposed that there was a continuous slow evolution of species on Earth. He was initially reluctant to publish his conclusions on human evolution, but he did so in 1871 when he published *The Descent of Man*.[6]

Many Christians did not accept Darwin's conclusions on human evolution since they seemed to disagree with what was in the Bible. It took about eighty years for the Catholic Church to acknowledge that there was no conflict between evolution and Christianity, which Pope Pius XII did in his encyclical *Humani generis*. The Pope stated that Christians need to believe that God created all things and that the soul specifically is created by God, not physical evolution.

Up until 1800 and even later, many scientists held religious beliefs and these did not inhibit their research. Galileo remained a devout Catholic for his entire life. Isaac Newton (1643–1727) held strong, but somewhat unorthodox religious beliefs.[7] Michael Faraday (1791–1867), an English scientist, who contributed to electromagnetism[8] and electrochemistry, was a devout Christian. James Clerk Maxwell (1831–79), who developed the classical theory of electromagnetic radiation, was an evangelical Presbyterian. Charles Darwin (1809–82), who is considered the father of evolution, initially was a Christian but his beliefs gravitated toward agnosticism as he aged. Albert Einstein (1879–1955) wrote: "Science without religion is lame, religion without science is blind."[9]

Numerous recent surveys show that contemporary scientists have lower religiosity in comparison to the general population. Rebecca McLaughlin gives a typical result that:

> 34 percent of science professors at elite universities say they do not believe in God, versus two percent of the general population, and a further 30 percent say they do not know if there is a God and there is no way to find out.[10]

---

5. Darwin, *Origin*.
6. Darwin, *Descent*.
7. Pfizenmaier, "Journal," 57–80.
8. Electromagnetism and electromagnetic radiation are discussed in Appendix A.
9. Einstein, *Ideas and Opinions*, 26.
10. McLaughlin, *Confronting Christianity*, 117.

Introduction and Goal of Book

A number of authors have discussed how to model the relationship between faith and science. Barbour[11] proposed four different models: conflict, independence, dialog, and integration. The conflict model posits that either science or faith must be wrong since both cannot be correct. Thus, the two are always in conflict. The independence model posits that both science and faith can be right as long as they stay within their respective domains. Since science involves physical facts while faith involves spiritual facts, the two domains are independent. The dialog model posits that faith and science can communicate with one another in any area where they both claim knowledge. Lastly, the integration model posits that the truths of faith and science can be integrated into a combined package.

Michael Guillen in his recent book *Believing Is Seeing* presents a very interesting perspective on the relationship between faith and science. Guillen, who has Ph.D. degrees in mathematics, physics, and astronomy, agrees that science restricts itself to the physical domain, but he points out that science actually requires faith! He presents examples of faith in mathematics, physics, astronomy, and the scientific method itself.

In his chapter on having faith in mathematics he states: "But as a mathematician myself, I assure you that there's no such thing as a faith-free proof. . . .Mathematics depends on beliefs that cannot be proven or imagined and, in many cases, are outright preternatural."[12] One example that Guillen gives is Euclid's definition of a point. He states: "Euclid defines a point as something with no width, no depth, and no length. It's both something and nothing! . . . A point doesn't make sense. It's not logical. It isn't even something you can see or imagine.[13] Thus, one has to take Euclid's definition of a point on faith. Guillen also discusses the fact that axioms, which are propositions that are regarded a self-evidently true, require faith since they are not proved, but accepted.

In his chapter on having faith in physics, Guillen discusses a number of Alice-in-Wonderland-like concepts that physicists have faith in. For example, photons have both wavelike and particle like characteristics. In so far as the location of an atom is concerned, Guillen states: "At any given moment, a typical atom is probably where classical physics says it should be. But you can't say it's there with complete confidence because it can be in many places simultaneously."[14] In our world we don't experience things simultaneously having dual natures or being in more than one place at the

---

11. Barbour, *When Science*, chap. 1.
12. Guillen, *Believing*, 105.
13. Guillen, *Believing*, 107.
14. Guillen, *Believing*, 127.

same time. In the microscopic world these aspects of matter are assumed possible based on faith.

Finally, with astronomy essentially all our knowledge is based on light measurements from space. However, Guillen points out that 95 percent of our universe consists of dark energy and dark matter, neither of which can be directly measured using light. As a result, he states: "That means that astronomers are forced to operate mostly in the dark. They must rely on faith to believe and defend their conjectures about our mostly invisible, otherworldly cosmos."[15]

I do not believe that faith and science are perpetually in conflict. In this book I approach faith and science principally from the perspective of the independence model. However, my approach also has aspects of the dialog and integration models. For example, consider the question of miracles, which involve physical facts that can be verified through investigation. Miracles are an area where dialog should occur.

Even though many scientists do not believe in miracles, their proper response to a miracle should be to examine the physical facts associated with it and verify their veracity. If an explanation for the facts cannot be given, then the proper scientific conclusion should be that science today cannot explain the physical facts. Scientists should not rule out from the start that miracles can occur, since a miracle is outside their domain of expertise. With this approach facts from faith and science can be integrated even though the two disciplines involve independent, non-overlapping domains.

Carl Sagan who was an agnostic and well-known astronomer and cosmologist has said: "Any faith that admires truth, that strives to know God, must be brave enough to accommodate the universe."[16] I interpret accommodate to mean to reconcile with faith and I fully agree with Sagan's statement.

My goal in writing this book is to show that scientific knowledge can support and enhance one's religious beliefs. A further goal is to attempt to present the scientific subjects that I cover in a way that they can be read and understood by someone who is not a scientist. Unfortunately, today when a non-scientist looks at science he/she can be bewildered by its complexity. I attempt to cut through that complexity in this book. I attempt to

---

15. Guillen, *Believing*, 140.
16. Sagan, *Contact*, 362.

Introduction and Goal of Book

present accurate scientific facts in a way that they can be understood by the non-scientist.

I am a firm believer in a Creator. Since my background is that of an engineer, I use an engineering perspective in this book. Without being presumptuous I ask how God might design a universe so that it could give rise to free, intelligent life. So that the reader does not get turned off by this design perspective, after discussing engineering design, I will give a simple example that illustrates my approach.

Although this book talks about the design of our universe, I want to strongly emphasize that the design that is discussed differs significantly from that proposed by the Intelligent Design (ID) movement. ID can correctly be described as follows:

> ID is a pseudoscientific argument for the existence of God, presented by its proponents as 'an evidence-based scientific theory about life's origins'. Proponents claim that 'certain features of the universe and of living things are best explained by an intelligent cause, not an undirected process such as natural selection [evolution].' ID is a form of creationism that lacks empirical support and offers no testable or tenable hypotheses, and is therefore not science.[17]

ID was established as an alternative to evolution. I believe that evolution teaches us a great deal about life as we know it and evolution and natural selection are fully compatible with faith in God. The design discussed in this book is backed up by facts that can be scientifically evaluated.

From my studies on cosmology, astronomy, physics, and evolution I am convinced that the universe certainly had a Designer. Indeed, Issac Newton believed that our universe had a Designer. A recent translation of Newton's *Principia Mathematica*, originally published in 1687, quotes Newton as: "This most elegant system of the Sun, planets, and comets could not have arisen without the design and dominion of an intelligent and powerful being."[18] Engineering design as a process inescapably involves tradeoffs. It is worthwhile to examine what is involved in an engineering design process, and then attempt to understand some of the issues involved with the design of the universe.

---

17. "Intelligent Design," para. 2.
18. Newton, *Principia*, 939–40.

God the Geometer

According to the text *Mechanical Engineering Design*, a *design imperative*[19] is the requirement to: "Design (subject to *problem-solving constraints*) a component, system, or process that will perform a specified task (subject to certain *solution constraints*) optimally."[20] The specified task is the *objective* or goal of the design and the parenthetical expressions refer to qualifications placed on the design. The *problem-solving constraints* involve what the designer knows or is able to do. The *solution constraints* involve issues like the design's functionality, safety, reliability, and conformity to standards and legal codes.

As an example, consider designing an automobile. The *objective* might be to design a car so that the maximum profit is made from selling it. To minimize *problem-solving constraints*, a company would want to employ top design engineers and have them make use of the best available automobile design software. For the automobile to be profitable a designer needs to consider a multitude of issues, including trying to minimize both manufacturing costs, leading to a low purchase price, and operating costs; both would make the car attractive to the public.

The automobile also has to have good styling so that the public will be inclined to purchase it. The final design has to be safe and perhaps meet governmental mileage efficiency standards. These are some of the considerations associated with *solution constraints*, and they lead to tradeoffs.

For good mileage one would want a light car, but for safety a heavier car could result in a better record when accidents occur. Without the economic *objective* of maximum profitability and the *solution constraints*, it would be easy to design an automobile so that the number of injuries and fatalities that resulted from accidents would be much, much less than they are today. One could make armor plated cars that could withstand high speed crashes. However, such automobiles would be very costly to purchase, and much less fuel efficient than those in use today. Designing a car that is as safe as possible and as fuel efficient as possible and that as many people as possible like and can afford, involves numerous tradeoffs. Indeed, essentially all products that the public uses today involve tradeoffs.

Now consider the design of our universe. In this design, God had to have an *objective* in mind, and there were *solution constraints* that had to

---

19. From here on in the book *design imperative* and its components will be printed in italics to point out to the reader the various scientific aspects of the design of our universe.

20. Shigley, *Mechanical*, 5.

Introduction and Goal of Book

be met. Since an all-knowledgeable God carried out the design there would be no *problem-solving constraints* in the *design imperative*. The *design imperative* and the *solution constraints* lead to tradeoffs in the final universe. Just what were the *objective* and the *solution constraints* in this design? This question is impossible to answer in a completely satisfying manner, given the complexity of the universe and our limited intelligence. We cannot put ourselves into God's mind and understand everything that he took into consideration in implementing his design. However, some aspects of the answer can be gotten by examining what we know from science about our universe today.

One *solution constraint* on the design was that it was a physical solution. As an alternative to physical creation, God could have designed humans to be pure spirits who would have been happy being in his presence. He did not design us in this manner, but rather used a physical creation with its built-in limitations. We know that our universe started with a Big Bang, and that the stars in our universe have a finite amount of fuel which eventually will be exhausted. When that happens life in the universe will definitely end, if not sooner. Infinity in our universe only exists as a mathematical extrapolation, but not as a practical fact. Thus, a physical world is constrained to be imperfect.

The facts presented in this book, based on cosmology, astronomy, physics, and evolution, demonstrate that the *objective* of the design was to produce a universe with intelligent life, *Homo sapiens,* that could evolve and be truly free. An indication of the freedom inherent in the universe can be gotten by considering the time scales involved with the Big Bang and evolution. The Big Bang occurred roughly 13.8 billion years ago, and the Earth has existed for roughly 4.5 billion years. *Homo sapiens*, which I believe is the primary *objective* of creation, has only been around for the last fifty thousand to one hundred thousand years (.0011–.0022% of time Earth existed). It took billions of years for stars and planets to form and evolution to generate intelligent life without outside interference. God was willing to wait a very long time for intelligence to emerge in the universe as it freely evolved.

I believe that God used an *autonomous design* in his *design imperative* to create the universe. Autonomous can be defined as: the quality or state of being independent, free, and self-directing. Once the Big Bang occurred God could sit back and let his creation freely develop on its own. An *autonomous design* has the tuning to achieve intelligent life built in from the start, and through physics and biological evolution God used a route to our creation that does not require his ongoing physical intervention.[21]

I believe that one important *solution constraint* is that the Creator wanted humans to be able to use their intelligence to see his presence in our universe. In a sense, an *autonomous design* camouflages the presence of the Designer. However, through the study of science humans have been able to see through the camouflage and ascertain God's presence in our world, just as he intended. In this book my goal is to explain a number of the important and amazing findings from science that support faith.

I believe that God's design allows humans the free will to affect outcomes on our planet. I also believe that physical miracles, due to God, occasionally happen, but they are very, very rare and by far the exception rather than the norm. Miracles for example might involve a person being cured of a disease but they do not involve changing the course of evolution on the Earth, as ID claims. When a miracle occurs, there is physical evidence for it that can be studied and evaluated scientifically. This situation stands in contrast to ID where no physical evidence exists.

I definitely do not believe that life is evolving in a purposeless, random manner, as some authors claim.[22] Rather the direction of evolution is toward free, intelligent life that can behave altruistically. God could have intervened, as proponents of ID claim, and speeded up the evolution process by directly creating some of the complicated biological systems we know about today.[23] The time scales cited above as well as evidence from evolution indicate that such intervention did not occur. The time scales indicate that the Creator did not want to be tweaking the universe and making physical changes to it. One can consider this limitation on intervention to be a *solution constraint* on the design.

The last word in the *design imperative*, namely optimally, indicates that the final design should be the best possible. Here we have to have faith that God created the very best universe in which humans could live, express their freedom, and have the opportunity to grow and be successful. In the following chapters a number of scientific areas are discussed and, in each chapter, the insights into God's design of our universe that can be gleaned from these areas are pointed out.

---

21. I believe that God regularly interacts with people on a spiritual level.
22. Dennett, *Darwin's*, 320.
23. "Intelligent Design," Intelligent Designer.

Introduction and Goal of Book

I believe that there is no conflict between faith and science, and that in fact knowledge of science can support one's faith. An interesting story presented by Father Andrew Apostoli in his book, *Fátima For Today The Urgent Marian Message Of Hope*, confirms this conclusion. An old man was sitting on a train in France saying his rosary. At a certain stop a university student got onto the train and sat near the old man. When the student noticed the rosary, he began to ridicule the old man saying: "Put that rosary away! We don't need prayer anymore! We're not dependent on God! We can run the world on our own; today we have science to control our destiny!"[24] The old man just sat there silently, continuing to pray his rosary. When he got up to leave the train, he reached into his pocket, took out a business card and gave it to the student. We can only imagine the surprise and shock on the face of the student when he read the card: Dr. Louis Pasteur—Academy of Sciences—Paris, France.[25]

Another insightful quote attributed to Pasteur (1822–95) which also supports my conclusion about science supporting faith is: "A little science estranges men from God, but much science leads them back to Him."[26] Based on my studies of cosmology, astronomy, physics, and evolution I think this statement is right on target. The more one looks at science the more one sees the hand of God.

In the following chapters, particularly chapters 2 to 4, a number of technical terms are used. These terms include: electromagnetic force, radiation, magnetic field, x-rays, ultraviolet, light, infrared, microwave, spectroscopy, radar, and the Doppler effect. To facilitate a non-scientist reading this book, Appendix A presents a discussion of these terms for the reader who may not be completely familiar with them. When other technical terms are used in the text, an explanation of them is given. Appendix B discusses proteins, and Appendix C discusses genetic algorithms, and both subjects are important for the discussion of evolution in chapters 5 and 6.

---

24. Apostoli, *Fátima*, 134.
25. Some have questioned the accuracy of this story.
26. Fanti, *Shroud*, 321.

2

The Big Bang

THE OPENING LINE OF the Apostles Creed is: "I believe in God, the Father almighty, Creator of heaven and Earth."[1] So how did God actually create heaven and Earth? Genesis, the first book of the Old Testament, starts with the story of the creation of the universe. In Genesis there are two creation stories; the first involves the days of creation and the second is the Adam and Eve story. Both stories say that God created the universe as well as humans, but neither is scientific. Thus, the Genesis creation stories contain important theology but not science. So, the question that arises is what does science say about the creation of our universe and how does that relate to one's faith?

The Big Bang is accepted today by the vast majority of scientists as the correct theory describing how our universe began. Simon Singh wrote a best-selling book,[2] *The Big Bang*, about the subject. Singh is an excellent writer who is able to make complex subject matter understandable to a non-scientist. I want to highlight some of the major points he makes to support the theory of a Big Bang beginning of our universe. For additional details about the Big Bang, the interested reader can consult Singh's book.

The Big Bang refers to what occurred when our universe was formed, approximately 13.8 billion years ago. The entire universe at the time of the

---

1. "Apostles," para. 1.
2. Singh, *Big*.

The Big Bang

Big Bang was contained in a very tiny volume, and there were no atoms or matter present at the start of the Big Bang. A recent article points out that The universe only contained an unbelievable amount of radiation[3] energy, and the temperature of the early universe just after the Big Bang has been estimated[4] to be an unbelievable 10^{32} degrees Centigrade[5] (°C) (100000000 000000000000000000000000 °C). By contrast the temperature of the Sun's core is about 15000000 °C. Once this initial universe was formed it began to expand rapidly like a balloon and this expansion continues to this day. Figure 2.1 shows a schematic diagram of this expansion.

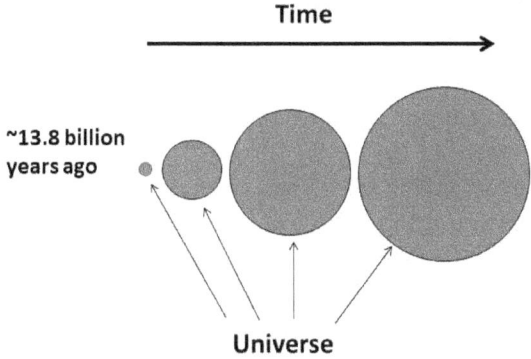

Figure 2.1. Expansion of universe after the Big Bang.

The major advance in understanding the beginning of our universe came with the theory of relativity. Einstein (1879–1955) published his special theory of relativity in 1905[6] and his general theory of relativity in 1915.[7] Einstein's theories provided a mathematical model that could be used to calculate the expansion of the universe.

After publishing his general theory of relativity, Einstein began to examine the cosmological implications of the theory. Einstein was troubled by the fact that if he applied his theory to the universe, it predicted that the universe would eventually collapse due to gravity. Einstein believed in a static, eternal universe, that neither expanded or contracted. To overcome

3. Radiation is an electromagnetic wave and it is discussed in Appendix A.
4. Singh, *Big*, 474–75.
5. Water boils at 100 degrees Centigrade.
6. Singh, *Big*, 108–16.
7. Singh, *Big*, 116–37.

the predicted collapse, he introduced a cosmological constant into his theory. This constant worked in a direction that was opposite to gravity and it resulted in a universe that did not collapse on itself.

A Russian mathematician, Alexander Friedmann, reexamined Einstein's relativity equations with and without the fix of the cosmological constant.[8] Friedmann demonstrated that there were three possible solutions to Einstein's relativity equations, and that one solution, without the cosmological constant, was a solution that changed with time; this solution resulted in a universe that would keep expanding forever. Independently, a Belgian priest and cosmologist, Father Georges Lemaitre, who was unaware of Friedmann's work, came to the same conclusion two years after Friedmann died. Although Einstein publicly criticized Lemaitre's work, later he was forced to admit that the mathematics was correct and that an expanding universe was one possible solution that was consistent with general relativity.

In order to determine whether the universe is expanding, contracting, or static, it is necessary to measure the distance to stars and their velocity relative to Earth. Singh gives a fascinating history of the development of such measurement techniques.[9] Edwin Hubble made the measurements that showed that our universe is expanding. First, to estimate a star's distance from the Earth, he used an approach developed by Henrietta Swan Leavitt in 1908. Leavitt worked at Harvard University around the turn of the twentieth century cataloguing stars. Leavitt's insights gave astronomers a method to measure distance on an intergalactic scale and Hubble used her formula to see outside our own Milky Way galaxy and into the universe beyond. A galaxy is a collection of stars that typically has a black hole at its center.

Hubble measured the light coming from stars of known distance and compared his measurements to the light coming from the Sun. The light from the stars exhibited a Doppler shift which occurs when an object (star) is moving relative to another object (Earth). One example of the Doppler shift is the sound effect you experience when you hear the change in pitch of an ambulance's siren as it moves either toward you or away from you. From Hubble's measurements a star's velocity relative to the Earth could be

---

8. Singh, *Big*, 149–56.
9. Singh, *Big*, chap. 3.

The Big Bang

calculated. Hubble's plot of a star's distance versus its velocity was published in 1929 and it is shown in Figure 2.2 below.[10]

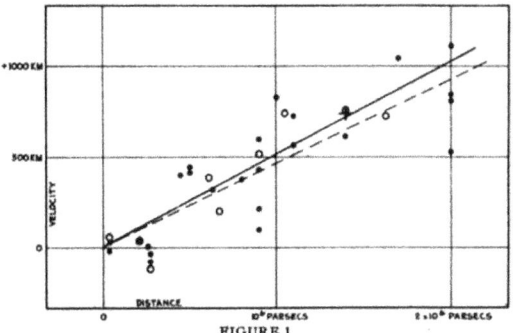

Figure 2.2. Hubble's distance-velocity plot for stars.

Distance is given by the x-axis, and velocity by the y-axis. The two straight lines are two models of the data that Hubble developed. The plot shows that the farther a star is from the Earth, then the faster it is moving away from the Earth. Indeed, Hubble found that a star's velocity was proportional to its distance from the Earth. Stars farther away have a higher velocity and move away faster than those closer by.

The fact that our universe is expanding is profound. However, there is a second and even more profound conclusion that can be drawn from Hubble's work. If one reverses time, the expansion process reverses, and all the stars and matter in the universe coalesce back to a very, very tiny volume. The temperature within the tiny volume occupied by the universe just after it began would be so enormously high that matter could not exist. Thus, only radiation energy existed at the beginning of our universe. The conclusion from reversing time is that there was a start to our universe, a creation moment! Measurements have shown that this creation moment occurred roughly 13.8 billion years ago.

Recent evidence has indicated that the Big Bang itself happened a very tiny fraction of second after our universe was created. Prior to the Big Bang there was an extremely short fraction of a second during which space inflated at an enormous rate and then the Big Bang occurred.[11] Given the

10. Hubble, "Proceedings," 168–73.
11. Siegel, "Strongest."

extreme brevity of this inflationary period, for all practical purposes the time of occurrence of the Big Bang is essentially the time when our universe was created. Physicists have carried out calculations about the state of our universe after the Big Bang occurred. These calculations indicate that the universe was so enormously hot that the largest particle accelerators currently available cannot begin to create the energies that existed then.[12]

Lederman[13] estimates that the particles that formed in the early stages of the Big Bang smashed into one another with energies that are a trillion (10^{12}) times higher than those achieved in the largest particle accelerators in use in 2006. Newer particle accelerators, such as the one run by Conseil Européen pour la Recherche Nucléaire (CERN) in Switzerland, do not change this situation. Thus, we lack basic knowledge about the physics of the dense, hot state that existed just after our universe began, and given the energies that are required to duplicate the earliest conditions, humans no doubt will never be able to study them experimentally on Earth. Thus, in trying to describe the universe just after the Big Bang, scientists have to have faith that they can extrapolate their knowledge to conditions that they will never be able to achieve experimentally here on Earth.

Before describing what happened in the first few minutes after the Big Bang, I want to briefly discuss atomic structure. This discussion is useful for illustrating some of the types of subatomic particles that existed after the Big Bang. Figure 2.3 gives a schematic diagram of an atom of deuterium, which is an isotope of hydrogen.

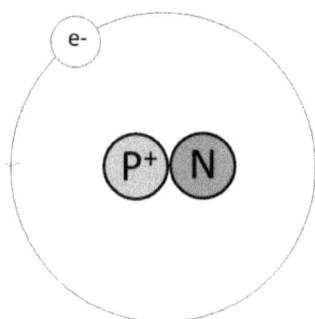

Figure 2.3. Schematic diagram of deuterium atom.

12. Rees, *Just*, 133.

13. Lederman, *God Particle*, 387.

The Big Bang

As shown in the diagram deuterium has 3 subatomic particles, a positively charged proton (P+) and a neutrally charged neutron (N) both in its nucleus. A negatively charged electron (e-) orbits the nucleus. An isotope of an element has the same number of protons in its nucleus but a different number of neutrons. Hydrogen has only a single proton and no neutron in its nucleus and one electron orbits its nucleus.

Protons and neutrons are composed of additional subatomic particles called quarks, while an electron is not so composed. Protons, neutrons, and electrons all have mass. A neutron is 1.0014 times heavier than a proton and 1839 times heavier than an electron. An atomic element is determined by the number of protons in its nucleus, which is matched by the number of orbiting electrons in order to keep an atom's net charge neutral. Nitrogen has seven protons in its nucleus and oxygen has eight protons. Numerous atomic elements have isotopes. For example, carbon, which has six protons and six electrons, has two stable isotopes, one with six neutrons in its nucleus and a second with seven neutrons in its nucleus.

To model the Big Bang theory, it was necessary to describe the state of the universe during the Big Bang using scientific knowledge available in the 1940s. Ralph Alpher a student of George Gamow developed such a model which described the universe after the Big Bang.[14] Alpher defended the model as part of his Ph.D. studies in 1948. The results predicted by the model are discussed next.

After the Big Bang, the universe expanded at an extremely fast rate, and as it expanded it cooled. After three minutes, the model estimated that the universe's temperature would have dropped to 10^9 °C (1000000000 °C). At this time subatomic building blocks which had mass, namely protons, neutrons, and electrons together with other particles would have existed. These building blocks resulted from the conversion of radiation energy to mass.

The fact that mass and energy can be converted to one another is shown by Einstein's famous relativity equation $E = mc^2$. E is energy, m is mass and c is the speed of light, which is an extremely large constant (186,000 miles/sec). This equation demonstrates that mass and energy are interrelated. A small amount of mass can be converted into an extremely large amount of energy, since c^2 (c squared) which multiplies m is so large. Alternatively, it takes a tremendous amount of energy to produce a small

---

14. Singh, *Big*, 306–36.

amount of mass. Conditions just after the Big Bang were so intense that no atoms were formed, but only the building blocks of atoms were formed.

A proton is the nucleus of the hydrogen atom. After the Big Bang protons and neutrons were also converted to charged deuterium nuclei and helium nuclei. The process of generating helium and deuterium nuclei from protons and neutrons is complex. This process involves nuclear fusion which can be described as follows:

> At a fundamental level, nuclear fusion is simply the process of bringing two or more protons, neutrons, or heavier nuclei made up of protons and neutrons together, under conditions that cause them to combine into a still-heavier nucleus, where a net amount of energy is released from the reaction.[15]

A recent example can be used to illustrate nuclear fusion. On December 5, 2022 Lawrence Livermore Lab announced that nuclear fusion had been achieved using lasers, where more energy was produced than was required to run the lasers.[16] Figure 2.4 gives a schematic diagram of the fusion reaction achieved in the lab.

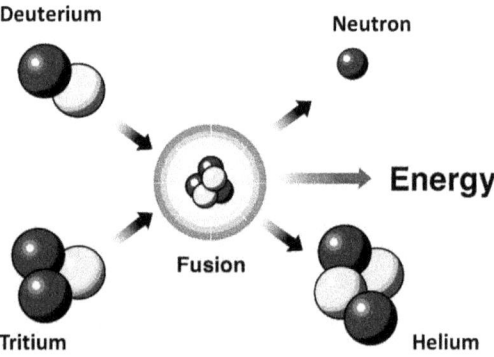

Figure 2.4. Fusion of hydrogen isotopes to helium DOE.[17]

In this case two hydrogen isotopes, deuterium and tritium, are forced together where their nuclei fuse producing a heavier helium atom, a neutron, and energy.

15. Siegel, "Why," para. 5.
16. Pearle, "What," para. 4.
17. Lanctot, "DOE," para. 1.

The Big Bang

Nuclear fusion is precisely what occurs in the Sun today, and it gives rise to the energy that the Sun releases. The fusion reactions that occur in the Sun are different than those that occurred just after the Big Bang because conditions, such as temperature and density, are different. The fusion reactions are also different from those achieved at Lawrence Livermore Lab. For the production of helium in our Sun the following very simplified equation shows the overall process which is actually very complex:[18]

4 protons → helium nucleus + energy + particles

Four protons react to produce one helium nucleus, plus particles, plus a significant amount of energy.[19]

Siegel[20] discusses the nuclear fusion reactions that took place just after the Big Bang. These reactions produced deuterium and helium nuclei, a very tiny amount of lithium nuclei, and radiation. All the nuclei are positively charged. Hydrogen is the lightest atomic element with one proton in its nucleus, helium is the second lightest element with two protons, and lithium is the third lightest element with three protons.

Just after the Big Bang no nuclei of elements heavier than lithium were produced through nuclear fusion. The reason that heavier nuclei were not formed is due to the fact that the initial expansion of the universe took place so fast that its mass density (mass per volume) decreased very rapidly. If mass density is too small, then there are not be enough collisions of lighter atomic nuclei for heavier nuclei to be produced through nuclear fusion. Nuclear fusion is critical for life to exist, and yet after about twenty minutes it stopped and as discussed below fusion did not begin again for millions of years! For approximately 380,000 years after the Big Bang, charged hydrogen nuclei, deuterium nuclei, helium nuclei, lithium nuclei, and electrons plus radiation were distributed throughout the universe.[21]

When the universe was about 380,000 years old, it had cooled to about 2700 °C, and neutral atoms of hydrogen and helium began to form. Formation occurred due to the electromagnetic force, discussed in Appendix A,

---

18. A more accurate but still simplified reaction is 6 protons → helium nucleus + 2 protons + 2 positrons + 2 neutrinos + energy. A positron is the positively charged anti-particle of the electron, and a neutrino is a particle. Two protons emerge from the reaction.

19. Siegel, "Why," para. 21.

20. Siegel, "Why."

21. Neutrino particles and dark matter, which is presently still a mystery, were also present.

when positively charged nuclei combined with negatively charged electrons. The next time you drink water which has one oxygen and two hydrogen atoms, think about the fact that the hydrogen atoms in it are approximately 13.8 billion years old. As discussed below oxygen atoms are millions of years younger than hydrogen atoms.

Alpher and Gamow used known information from atomic physics to calculate the ratio of hydrogen to helium that would be produced as a result of the Big Bang. Their result was in very close agreement with what is measured in today's universe, namely an approximately ten to one ratio of hydrogen atoms to helium atoms.[22] Alpher and Gamow's model was not able to explain the formation of the many heavier atomic elements, e.g. carbon, oxygen, iron, etc., and this fact was a limitation of their research.

A key result of Alpher's research involved what happened to the radiation that was not converted into mass during the first twenty minutes after the Big Bang. This radiation was an electromagnetic wave that normally travels in a straight line. However, as long as charged particles, particularly electrons, were present in the universe (for 380,000 years) the radiation followed a zig zag path as it collided and interacted with the charged particles. Once neutral atoms were formed, the collisions between the radiation and the neutral atoms essentially stopped. Radiation was then free to travel in a straight line. Siegel[23] gives an excellent discussion on these points.

During the 380,000 years where the radiation collided and interacted with the charged particles, the radiation took on a particular frequency distribution, called a black body distribution. As a result of the expansion of the universe over 13.8 billion years, the distribution of the left-over radiation was shifted toward the microwave frequency range. Alpher and Herman wrote a short paper[24] in 1948 in which they estimated the temperature of the shifted radiation to be 5 degrees Kelvin (°K).[25] In 1992 NASA launched the COsmic Background Explorer satellite (COBE) to measure the radiation left over from the Big Bang. Figure 2.5 gives a plot of the data measured by COBE and the distribution curve for black body radiation.

---

22. On a mass basis approximately a ratio of two and one half to one hydrogen to helium, since helium is four times heavier than hydrogen.

23. Siegel, "How."

24. Alpher, "Nature," 774–75.

25. °K is equal to °C+273.15. The lowest possible temperature is °K = 0, called absolute zero.

The Big Bang

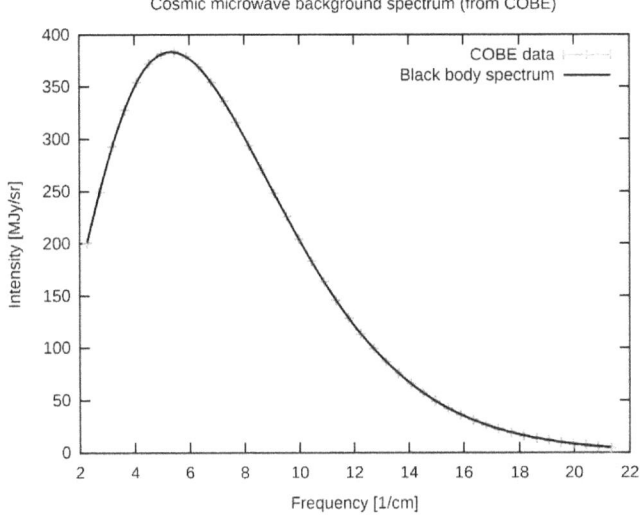

Figure 2.5. CBOE data and black body spectrum.[26]

The temperature associated with the black body spectrum in Figure 2.5 is 2.73 °K and the fit to the measured data is excellent. Given when Alpher and Herman's calculation was carried out, their estimate of 5 °K for the temperature of the cosmic background radiation is impressive. The excellent agreement between the COBE data and the Big Bang model proposed by Alpher and Gamow is a key result that has helped convince the vast majority of scientists of the validity of the Big Bang theory.

The first stars formed via gravity about one hundred million years after the Big Bang. The difference between the time for the formation of neutral atoms, 380,000 years, and the time for formation of the first stars, around one hundred million years, reflects the weakness of the gravitational force compared to the electromagnetic force.[27] The first stars consisted essentially of hydrogen and helium and they burned for billions of years. Due to gravity, the mass density in stars is high enough for nuclear fusion to take place at the temperatures inside the stars. For much of their life early stars fused hydrogen into helium.

---

26. "CMBR"
27. The difference also is partially due to the ongoing expansion of the universe.

God the Geometer

Singh provides a fascinating discussion of how Fred Hoyle proposed a theory[28] that heavier atomic elements were produced in stars. When early, large stars used up their hydrogen fuel and began to die, they contracted, and their core heated up, resulting in the fusion of helium into carbon, oxygen, and other heavy atoms.[29] This process does not happen in our Sun yet, but it will happen when our Sun exhausts its supply of hydrogen fuel, contracts, and heats up as it begins to die.

Even approaching death, stars burn for a very long time, which was enough to allow the formation of the heavier atoms within them via fusion of lighter atoms. When early stars died, the heavier atoms were ejected into the star's surroundings. Then, when second generation stars formed via gravity, they incorporated not only hydrogen and helium but heavier atoms that had been ejected as well. Through gravity, the heavier atoms also formed planets. Atoms heavier than hydrogen and helium constitute less than 1 percent of the mass in the universe. Our Sun is a third-generation star.

The biggest problem with Hoyle's theory involved the production of carbon. In 1953 he predicted that an excited, resonance state of carbon, that had not yet been measured experimentally, had to exist. Hoyle's prediction is discussed in more detail in chapter 3. In making his prediction, Hoyle was trying to explain the abundance of carbon in the universe. Indeed, shortly after he made his prediction, this excited state was measured. Since carbon is absolutely essential to life on Earth and since it was not formed in the Big Bang itself, Hoyle's prediction was critical to explaining carbon's existence.

Ironically, Hoyle himself did not believe in the Big Bang theory; he was a proponent of a competing Steady State theory of the universe. It was he who actually coined the phrase Big Bang as a derisive term. Both the Big Bang and Steady State theories needed an explanation for the production of atomic elements heavier than helium, and this need was the reason Hoyle looked into how heavier atoms might be produced. It is interesting to realize that our bodies and just about all the things we see around us were made from atoms in stars that died. An optimist would say that humans and everything we see on Earth are made from stardust. A pessimist would claim we are built from nuclear waste.

---

28. Singh, *Big*, 386–96.
29. "Atom," para. 8.

The Big Bang

In 1964 two Bell Laboratory scientists, Robert Wilson and Arno Penzias, were scanning the skies for radio sources using an antenna from a discontinued project.[30] They discovered a background noise that appeared to come from everywhere in space. At first the two researchers thought that the noise might be coming from the equipment they were using. However, it turned out that their equipment was not the problem. The background noise was radiation, now labeled cosmic microwave background (CMB) radiation. Most people are familiar with using a microwave oven to heat food. The oven uses the same type of radiation present in CMB radiation, but the oven radiation is much, much stronger than the CMB radiation, i.e. there is a lot more of it in an oven.

Eventually, Wilson and Penzias became aware that Alpher and Gamow's theory predicted that radiation would have resulted from the Big Bang. If a television is tuned to a channel which does not have an input signal from either a cable box or an antenna, a sizeable amount of the resulting static that is heard is caused by the CMB radiation produced in the Big Bang. The two Bell Laboratory researchers, who won a Nobel Prize for their discovery, had stumbled onto a measurement that corroborated the Big Bang theory.

There are a number of insights into God's *design imperative* for our universe that can be gleaned from the Big Bang. First, as pointed out above in the very first line of the Old Testament book of Genesis it is stated that God created heaven and Earth. There was nothing prior to God's creation and it is therefore labeled ex nihilo, i.e. from nothing. The Big Bang is consistent with ex nihilo creation. Before the Big Bang and the short inflationary period preceding it there was nothing and then the universe began.

A second insight into God's *design imperative* comes from the truly amazing fine-tuning of physical forces and constants in our universe. At least 10 of these forces and constants have values which cannot be altered very much without life on Earth being impossible. This fine-tuning is so important that it is addressed in detail in chapter 3. In the epilogue to *The Big Bang* Singh comments on a book which discusses six fine-tuned constants, entitled *Just Six Numbers*,[31] by Martin Rees. Singh states:

> It seems to defy odds that the six numbers that characterize the universe have very special values that allow life to flourish. So, do

---

30. Singh, *Big*, 425–37.
31. Rees, *Just*.

God the Geometer

we ignore this and just count ourselves extremely lucky or do we look for *special meaning* in our extraordinary good fortune?[32]

A third insight into God's *design imperative* can be gotten by examining the energy implications of the Big Bang. It is almost impossible to comprehend the amount of energy involved in the Big Bang. The amount of energy that would have been required to generate the mass in our universe has to be divided by c^2, since $m=E/c^2$. As discussed above c is 186,000 miles/sec, and squaring c results in an extremely large number. In atomic explosions mass is converted to energy, while in the Big Bang the reverse occurs and energy is converted to mass, but $E = mc^2$ holds for both.

The atomic bomb dropped on Nagasaki contained fourteen pounds of plutonium, of which less than one gram was converted to energy. The amount of mass converted was equal to one third of the mass in a penny. Over forty thousand lives were instantly lost and as shown in Figure 2.6 many buildings in Nagasaki were leveled.

Figure 2.6. Nagasaki after the atomic bomb explosion.[33]

If one gram of mass could generate this much energy, consider the enormous amount of energy that would be required to make the atoms in your hand, your arm, or your body, all of which weigh considerably more than one gram. If the mass of your arm could be converted to energy it would be more than enough to destroy a city the size of New York, and probably much of the State of New York and surrounding states! Fortunately, once

32. Singh, *Big*, 486–87.
33. "Nagasaki."

The Big Bang

stable atoms are formed they cannot be converted back to energy. Only unstable radioactive atoms like uranium can be converted into energy via nuclear fission. Nuclear fission differs from nuclear fusion in that fission involves breaking atoms into smaller components, while fusion builds up atoms from smaller components.

Consider further how much energy would be required to make the atoms in the Earth, or the atoms in our solar system, or in our galaxy. Since it is estimated that there are two hundred billion galaxies in our universe, the amount of energy involved in their creation is the closest thing to infinity that one can imagine. This enormous amount of energy is the reason the initial temperature just after the Big Bang has been estimated to be 10^{32} °C. The insight that the Big Bang energy gives into God's power and majesty is truly awe inspiring.

A fourth insight into God's *design imperative* comes from the very large time scales involved. Our Sun formed roughly 4.6 billion years ago, and it is estimated that the Sun will burn for about another five billion years. As discussed in chapters 5 and 6 evolution is a very slow process. The time scale for our Sun producing energy is perfectly matched to the very slow and incredible evolutionary process that led to humans.

3

Fine-Tuning in the Universe

FROM ROUGHLY 1950 UNTIL 1970 the Big Bang and Steady State theories of the creation of our universe competed with one another. An advantage of the Big Bang theory was that it could predict the approximately ten to one ratio of hydrogen atoms to helium atoms in the universe, whereas the Steady State theory could not.

In 1964 Robert Wilson and Arno Penzias made the first measurement of the cosmic microwave background radiation (CMB) produced by the Big Bang. Then in 1989 NASA launched a cosmic background explorer (COBE) satellite that made detailed measurements of the CMB in 1992, and that measurement validated the Big Bang theory. It was the death knell for the Steady State theory.

During the mid-1900s while the debate about the Big Bang versus the Steady State theories was going on, physicists began to realize that very small changes to the fundamental constants of nature would rule out life as we know it. Perhaps the earliest publication that discussed fine-tuning in our universe was a 1961 letter to the editors of the journal *Nature* written by Dicke.[1] We live in a universe that supports intelligent human life, i.e. an anthropic universe, as well as other life. What physicists have discovered is that very small changes to any of a significant number of physical constants

---

1. Dicke, "Nature," 440–41.

Fine-Tuning in the Universe

would result in a non-anthropic universe, i.e. one that does not support human life. The number of fine-tuned constants is greater than ten.

Father Robert Spitzer is a Jesuit scholar with a truly amazing knowledge of physics, philosophy, and theology. In his book, *New Proofs for the Existence of God*, Father Spitzer discusses cosmological fine-tuning in depth. He concludes: "it would seem that the immensity of the difference between anthropic and non-anthropic values of our universal constants provides reasonable and responsible rationale for belief in supernatural design."[2] It is interesting that Father Spitzer uses the word design.

Father Spitzer discusses seven instances of the narrow range of constants necessary for our anthropic universe to exist. Some of the instances discussed require a detailed knowledge of physics. Assuming that a non-scientist does not have such knowledge, only two of Father Spitzer's instances are discussed below. After the discussion of these two instances, a discussion of two additional examples of fine-tuning in our universe, given by other authors, is presented.

One of the seven instances involves what is called the strong nuclear force. As discussed in chapter 2, all atoms contain a nucleus that consists of positively charged protons and neutrally charged neutrons contained in a nucleus orbited by negatively charged electrons. Figure 3.1 gives a schematic diagram of an atom of helium.

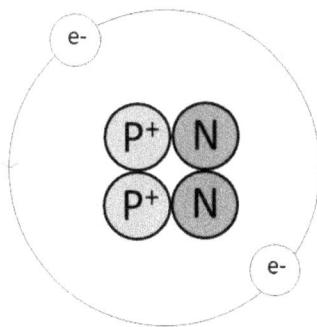

Figure 3.1. Schematic diagram of helium atom.

As can be seen, helium has two protons in its nucleus together with two neutrons. As a result of their like charge, the protons try to repel one

2. Spitzer, *New*, 67.

another, just as two magnets repel one another when their two like poles are pushed together. The fundamental force that holds protons together in the nucleus of an atom is called the strong nuclear force. This force has a very significant effect on the process of forming larger atoms from smaller atoms inside stars through nuclear fusion.

As discussed by Father Spitzer,[3] if the strong nuclear force had been about two percent weaker no heavy atomic elements, e.g., oxygen, carbon, iron, could have formed in the fusion process within stars. As a result, life which requires these heavy atoms would not be possible. If the strong nuclear force had been two percent stronger, too much hydrogen would have been transformed into helium in the very early universe, and there would not have been enough hydrogen left to fuel stars. With no stars there would be no atoms that are required for life. Life as we know it could not exist, and the conclusion is that the strong nuclear force has to have tight bounds for an anthropic universe to exist.

A second instance of the tight range of constants for an anthropic universe involves the relationship between the electromagnetic[4] and gravitational force constants, and the ratio of the electron to proton mass. A proton's mass is 1,836 times the mass of an electron. The electromagnetic force involves the interaction between electrically charged moving particles. Inside a common magnet there are moving electrons that carry an electrical charge, and thereby generate a magnetic force field. In magnets the electrons move in the same direction thereby generating a magnetic field. In non-magnet materials the electrons move in opposite directions and as a result their magnetic fields are cancelled.

All of us experience the force of gravity and we tend to think of it as a strong force. Gravity, in fact, is extremely weak when compared to the electromagnetic force. The electromagnetic force is 10^{36} (1 with 36 zeroes after it) times stronger than the force of gravity. When we experience gravity, we are feeling the pull of the entire mass of the Earth on our body. Since the Earth is so large compared to us, the gravitational force generated by it appears to be large.

Now consider pulling two small magnets apart. Even if the magnets are small one can feel the force they exert on each other. Consider the

---

3. Spitzer, *New*, 61–62.

4. The electromagnetic force is not as familiar to nonscientists as is the gravitational force. Appendix A explains the electromagnetic force and gives examples of its use in everyday life.

Fine-Tuning in the Universe

hypothetical case where we had two magnets each the size of ½ the Earth, so together they would equal the size of Earth. Now imagine trying to pull the magnets apart. Due to the strength of the electromagnetic force holding the magnets together, it would be essentially impossible to separate such large magnets. To do the separation an enormous force would be required. Although hypothetical this discussion illustrates just how strong the electromagnetic force is.

In discussing the second instance Father Spitzer quotes Professor Paul Davies, a well-known researcher and cosmologist, as: "If gravity were very slightly weaker, or electromagnetism very slightly stronger, (or the electron slightly less massive relative to the proton), all stars would be red dwarfs. A correspondingly tiny change the other way, and they all would be blue giants."[5] Importantly, neither red dwarfs nor blue giants are likely capable of sustaining life as we know it. This point is discussed in detail in chapter 4 on the fine-tuning aspects of our solar system. Our Sun is G-type star, also called a yellow dwarf star, and it is capable of sustaining life on Earth. Father Spitzer concludes:

> the anthropic values for these four constants [Gravity and electromagnetism, proton and electron masses] have a very narrow closed range while non-anthropic values have an open, almost indefinite range, making the emergence of stable stars necessary for the development of life forms exceedingly improbable.[6]

Another example of fine-tuning involves Fred Hoyle, who coined the phrase Big Bang in 1949. Fred declared himself an atheist at the time. One of the nuclear fusion results that Hoyle contributed very significantly to involved an excited, resonance state of carbon, now called the Hoyle state.[7] The fine-tuning involved in the Hoyle state is discussed below, after discussing the history of the Hoyle state. One of Father Spitzer's seven fine-tuning instances involves the Hoyle state.

Recall that carbon was not created in the Big Bang, but rather it was created much later in stars and expelled into the universe when the stars died. Hoyle realized that what was known in the early 1950s about nuclear fusion could not explain the abundance of carbon in the universe. In 1953 he predicted that a resonance state of carbon, which had not yet been

---

5. Spitzer, *New*, 63.
6. Spitzer, *New*, 63.
7. "Carbon," para. 4.

measured experimentally, had to exist.[8] If the resonance state of carbon did not exist, then carbon would be rare in our universe. Indeed, after he made his prediction, the excited, resonance state of carbon was measured shortly afterwards and a paper on the measurement was published in 1957.[9]

Hoyle was not a co-author on the 1957 paper. One of the paper's authors, Willy Fowler, won the 1983 Nobel Prize for the measurement. Fowler was astounded that Hoyle, who had come up with the key insight for his experiment, was not named as a joint winner of the Nobel Prize. Fowler wrote to Hoyle and said that he could not understand why Hoyle was not so named. Hoyle was outspoken and at times somewhat abrasive. He had criticized the Nobel Prize committee about an earlier award and he was engaged in research on the controversial issue that life began in outer space and not on Earth. One or both of these issues may have contributed to the slight by the Nobel Prize committee.

The Hoyle state is difficult to describe in simple terms. The numerical value of the Hoyle state has been measured as 7.656 mega electronvolts (MeV). An electron volt is a unit of energy used in high energy physics, and a mega electron volt is one million electron volts. According to one calculation:

> if the [Hoyle] state's energy level were lower than 7.3 or greater than 7.9 MeV, insufficient carbon would exist to support life. Furthermore, to explain the universe's abundance of carbon, the Hoyle state must be further tuned to a value between 7.596 and 7.716 MeV[10]

a range of ±0.78%.

In 1982 after much further study Hoyle stated:

> A common sense interpretation of the facts suggests that a superintellect has monkeyed with physics, as well as with chemistry and biology, and that there are no blind forces worth speaking about in nature. The numbers one calculates from the facts seem to me so overwhelming as to put this conclusion almost beyond question.[11]

So, Hoyle came around to the idea that there was a superintellect behind the creation of the universe. Believers call this superintellect God.

8. Kragh, "Archive," 721–51.
9. Cook, "Physical," 508.
10. "Fine," para. 11.
11. Hoyle, "Engineering," 8–12.

Fine-Tuning in the Universe

A fourth example of fine-tuning involves Martin Rees, an astrophysicist and cosmologist. He published a book, *Just Six Numbers*,[12] in which he considers the magnitude of six physical constants associated with the Big Bang. Rees concludes that if any of these six constants had slightly different values, life as we know it would have been impossible. Two of the constants discussed by Rees are the same as those discussed above in Father Spitzer's two instances. Here I will consider a third constant, discussed by Rees, that has to be fine-tuned for life to exist.

The third constant involves a ratio of densities of mass in the universe. Density involves mass per volume. For example, the density of water is .0361 pounds per cubic inch and that of lead is .409 pounds per cubic inch, roughly eleven times greater than that of water. Rees' third constant is given the symbol Ω, and it is the ratio of the actual mass density in the universe to a critical mass density that can be calculated.

The value of Ω had a profound effect on the expansion of the universe after the Big Bang. If Ω were too small, then according to Rees: "galaxies and stars would never have been able to pull themselves together via gravity and condense out; the universe would expand forever, but there would be no chance of life."[13] If Ω were too large, the expansion would be too slow and the universe would collapse on itself in what he calls a Big Crunch. For either of these events not to have occurred, a remarkably narrow range for Ω is required. As Rees states: "the required precision is astonishing: at one second after the Big Bang, Ω cannot have differed from unity by more than one part in a million billion (one in 10^{15}) in order that the universe should now . . . still be expanding."[14]

Additional citations could be given to publications that demonstrate the fine-tuned nature of our universe. Suffice it to say that essentially all scientists, whether they are believers or not, recognize this fine-tuning. I chose to highlight Rees' book because he is an atheist. His reaction to our fine-tuned universe is typical of the reaction of non-believing scientists, when forced to face the facts of our universe. In particular these non-believing scientists have two significant problems:

Problem 1. The fine-tuning associated with the Big Bang.

Problem 2. The fact that the Big Bang indicates a beginning to our universe.

12. Rees, *Just*.
13. Rees, *Just*, 34.
14. Rees, *Just*, 34.

God the Geometer

As Fred Hoyle concluded, the fine-tuning must have resulted from a superintellect behind creation, and non-believing scientists do not like this conclusion.

As a starting point to overcome problem 1, many scientists immediately rule out the possibility of God creating our universe. Thus, many of these scientists have postulated that our universe is one universe in an almost infinite number of other universes, the so-called multiverse. These additional universes would have different values for their key physical constants, and therefore essentially all of them would not support life as we know it. For non-believing scientists the multiverse provides an answer to the infinitesimally small probably of our universe having the fine-tuning that it has. With an almost infinite number of universes one of them would have physical constants that support life. Rees subscribes to this multiverse hypothesis.

One problem with the multiverse hypothesis is that at present these additional universes are not observable from our universe, and they may never be observable. No measurements can be made on them. Thus, in a very real sense non-believing scientists have "faith" that the multiverse exists, since they don't believe God exists. To me it makes so much more sense to believe that God created the one universe that we know exists and that is fine-tuned for life as we know it. I have thought about how much non-believing scientists would ridicule a believer, if the situation were reversed and the believer's faith required an almost infinite number of universes, and atheism required only one.

Professor Paul Davies believes in God, but subscribes to no particular religion. In his 2003 *New York Times* opinion piece Davies offered a variety of arguments why multiverse theories are non-scientific:

> For a start, how is the existence of the other universes to be tested? To be sure, all cosmologists accept that there are some regions of the universe that lie beyond the reach of our telescopes, but somewhere on the slippery slope between that and the idea that there is an infinite number of universes, credibility reaches a limit. As one slips down that slope, more and more must be accepted on faith, and less and less is open to scientific verification. Extreme multiverse explanations are therefore reminiscent of theological discussions. Indeed, invoking an infinity of unseen universes to explain the unusual features of the one we do see is just as ad hoc as invoking an unseen Creator. The multiverse theory may be

Fine-Tuning in the Universe

dressed up in scientific language, but in essence, it requires the same leap of faith.[15]

I fully agree with his analysis and conclusions.

To overcome problem 2 many scientists have developed a number of mathematically sophisticated models of the universe. For example, one model involves a bouncing universe which has experienced many cycles of expansion (Big Bangs) and contraction (Big Crunches) in the past, perhaps even an infinite number. Most of these sophisticated models are much too complex to be discussed in this book.

In chapter 1 of his book, *New Proofs for the Existence of God*,[16] Father Spitzer presents an excellent discussion of the sophisticated models of the universe that have been proposed. He also discusses a theorem that applies to just about all of these models, including the multiverse and bouncing universe models. This theorem rules out that many of these models could be associated with an eternal universe, but rather the universes they model had to have a beginning.

Father Spitzer lays out four major conditions that any model of a universe would have to satisfy in order that the universe it describes not have a beginning. These four conditions are that: (1) the model has consistency with cosmological observation; (2) the model has internal consistency; (3) the model not be subject to the theorem that indicates it had a beginning; and (4) it avoids three additional technical conditions. He concludes:

> Perhaps one day physicists will be able to construct a model which meets all these [four] conditions. Yet accomplishing this does not mean that the model will resemble (or even remotely resemble) reality. Just because a hypothetical proposal meets the above [four] conditions does not mean that it corresponds to the past and present nature of the universe. Therefore, the hypothesis may only be a testimony to human ingenuity.[17]

Father Spitzer's discussion essentially obliterates the arguments that our universe did not have a beginning.

This chapter has discussed the fine-tuning of the physical constants in our universe. One can speculate about why God would use a *design imperative* that included this fine-tuning. One possible insight is that God wanted

---

15. Davies, "Brief," para. 10.
16. Spitzer, *New*.
17. Spitzer, *New*, 43–44.

humans to be able to discover the fine-tuning and to thereby see his hand in creation. Indeed, over the last one hundred and twenty years humans have been able to uncover and describe the universe's fine-tuning in amazing detail. It is this fine-tuning that has convinced Hoyle, Davies, and many other scientists that there was an intelligence behind the creation of our universe. The fine-tuning is also necessary for the long life of stars that then can support the very slow process of the evolution of life, discussed in chapters 5 and 6.

Another insight into God's *design imperative* is that it is reasonably certain that he did not create a universe that was either imbedded into a very complex multiverse or some other exotic system like a bouncing universe. While our universe is complex, its fine-tuning can be discovered and it shows God's fingerprints in its creation. As a result, having faith in God makes much more sense than having faith in some hypothetical and/or unobservable model of the universe.

Not only is our universe fine-tuned for life to exist, but our solar system is also fine-tuned for life. This solar system fine-tuning is discussed in the next chapter.

4

Fine-Tuning in Our Solar System

WARD AND BROWNLEE'S EXCELLENT book, *Rare Earth*[1], addresses Simon Singh's question about whether we are lucky to exist, discussed at the end of chapter 2. The first eight chapters discuss how cells and life could have evolved on Earth, starting with its early history. The next two chapters, which I consider in this chapter, discuss the Earth, our Moon, and solar system. Ward and Brownlee's arguments are based on scientific facts that demonstrate the fine-tuning of our planet and solar system, and they support the argument for a Creator.

Our solar system consists of our Sun and the eight planets (Mercury, Venus, Earth, Mars, Jupiter, Saturn, Uranus, and Neptune in order of distance from the Sun) revolving around it. The four inner planets are solid, rocky planets, while the four outer planets are large and composed primarily of gaseous hydrogen and helium. Figure 4.1A illustrates the differences in size of the among the planets in our solar system.

---

1. Ward, *Rare*.

Figure 4.1. Our Solar System. A relative size of planets.
B Distance from Sun from Wikipedia.[2]

As can be seen the Earth is small compared to the other planets. In Figure 4.1B the distance of the planets from the Sun is shown. The Earth is 91.5 million miles away from the Sun. Figure 4.1B also illustrates the immense size of the Sun compared to the planets in our solar system. The mass of the Sun constitutes 99.8 percent of the mass in our solar system. The Earth is so tiny compared to the Sun that it is just a tiny dot in Figure 4.1B.

In the universe there are billions of stars, and many of them have planets rotating around them. Many people think that surely there must be life on many of these planets; further many people feel that there is certainly nothing unique about our own solar system in general and the Earth in particular.

The facts given in *Rare Earth* counter these opinions. Ward and Brownlee show that while primitive life such as bacteria may be common, complex life such as humans is almost certainly uncommon. Some of the key arguments in *Rare Earth* are given in this chapter. For additional information the interested reader can consult *Rare Earth*.

Stars exist in galaxies and there are four major types of galaxies in the universe, spiral, elliptical, peculiar, and irregular.[3] Our galaxy, the Milky

2. "Solar."
3. Andersen, "AstroFan," Types of Galaxies.

Fine-Tuning in Our Solar System

Way, is a spiral galaxy, and our Sun resides far out from the Milky Way's center. According to NASA: "Stars in the arms of spiral galaxies [far out from the galaxy center] move in an orderly fashion around the center of the galaxy."[4] Figure 4.2 illustrates an almost circular orbit of a solar system in a spiral galaxy such as our solar system moving in the Milky Way.

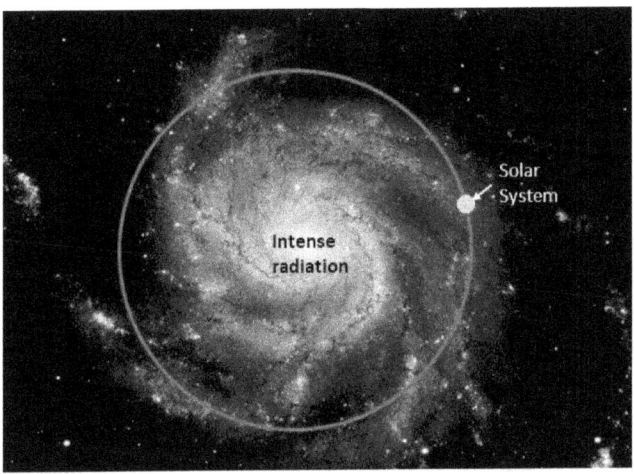

Figure 4.2. Almost circular solar system orbit in a spiral galaxy. ESA/Hubble.[5]

As can be seen our solar systems' orbit keeps it far away from the Milky Way's center.

At the center of most if not all galaxies is a black hole. Black holes have a large, dense mass in a very small volume and their gravitational pull is enormous. They are called black holes since they are so dense that light cannot escape from them. Any matter that comes near a black hole is attracted to it by its strong gravitational force. As matter is attracted it speeds up, and a large amount of radiation is emitted during the process. If the matter gets too close to the black hole it eventually gets swallowed up by it.

Stars near the center of a galaxy but far enough away from the black hole can survive its gravitational pull. However, these stars are subject to much more radiation than stars far away from the center of a galaxy. Since radiation is not conducive to life, it is good for humans that our Sun does not orbit near the center of our galaxy. We are fortunate that our galaxy is a spiral galaxy and that our solar system's galactic orbit is almost circular,

4. "Hidden," para. 1.
5. "Spiral."

so that the Earth does not get near the intense radiation in the center of the Milky Way. Both our solar system's galactic orbit and its distance from the Milky Way's center are two examples of the fine-tuning of our solar system.

NASA also states: "Stars in elliptical galaxies move in all directions. Stars in irregular galaxies move more or less in random fashion."[6] For peculiar galaxies NASA states: "Peculiars are not fundamentally a different type. They are simply galaxies [spiral, irregular, elliptical] in the act of colliding; the collision distorts their shape and makes them appear 'peculiar.'"[7]

In the case of elliptical and irregular galaxies, stars and their orbiting planets have orbits that cause them to visit the centers of their galaxies, where they can be exposed to the dangerous levels of radiation. Having a star in a spiral galaxy, and not in either an elliptical or irregular galaxy, is one of the criteria that *Rare Earth* uses for an orbiting planet to develop complex life.[8]

Henry and Worthey have pointed out that: "galaxies, on average, have heavy element abundances (metallicities) that systematically decrease outward from their galactic centers."[9] Metallicity refers to more than metals. It is the proportion of the material of a star that is in elements other than hydrogen or helium. More of the heavy atomic elements needed for life, e.g. carbon, oxygen, iron, etc., are available near the center of galaxies.

Far from the center of a galaxy, heavy atomic elements resulting from the death of earlier stars are not found in the same abundance as near the center, so the chances for the existence of Earth-like planets becomes less the farther away its star is from a galaxy's center. In this regard we are very fortunate not only that even though our solar system's location is far from our galaxy's center, that we have enough heavier atomic elements to support complex life.

Ward and Brownlee have an interesting discussion on the metallicity content of stars and its connection to planet formation. They state:

> According to astronomers conducting these studies, there seems to be a causal link between high metal content in a star and the presence of planets. In a study of 174 stars . . . the Sun was among the highest in metal content. It appears that we orbit a rare Sun."[10]

6. "Hidden," para. 1.
7. "Visible," para. 7.
8. Ward, *Rare*, xxxii.
9. Henry, "Publications," 919–45.
10. Ward, *Rare*, 268–69.

Fine-Tuning in Our Solar System

Our Sun's metallicity is another example of the fine-tuning in our solar system.

There are seven different types of stars in our universe and Table 4.1 shows the abundance of four of these types.[11]

Star Type	Color	Surface Temperature Range °K	Prevalence %
B	Blue	10,000—30,000	.13
G	Yellow	5,000—6,000	7.6
K	Orange	3,500—5,000	12.1
M	Red	< 3500	76.5

Table 4.1 Star types and properties (°C = °K—273)

Type-O stars, also called blue giants, are rare and they only constitute .13 percent of stars in our universe. The hotter a star is the rarer it is, and because of their high temperature blue giants use up their fuel and they die out very quickly compared to other stars. Blue giant stars only burn for a few hundred million years.

Type-G stars, also called yellow dwarfs, constitute 7.6 percent of the stars in our universe. Our Sun is a type-G star and it is estimated that it will burn for approximately nine to ten billion years. Type-K stars, also called orange dwarfs, constitute 12.1 percent of the stars in our universe. Orange dwarf stars can burn for tens of billions of years.

Type-M stars, also called red dwarfs, are the most numerous in our universe and the smallest class of stars that fuse hydrogen into helium. Type-M stars constitute 76.5 percent of the stars in our universe and they have the lowest temperature of any stars. A red dwarf star can burn for ten trillion years. The mass of red dwarf stars is between 0.08 and 0.6 the mass of our Sun.[12]

According to Wikipedia:

> Modern evidence suggests that planets in red dwarf systems are extremely unlikely to be habitable. In spite of their great numbers and long lifespans, there are several factors which may make life difficult on planets [revolving] around a red dwarf. First, planets

---

11. "Types," para. 4.
12. Gregersen, "Red Dwarf", para. 2.

in the habitable zone of a red dwarf would be so close to the parent star that they would likely be tidally locked.[13]

The habitable zone is the distance from a star at which liquid water could exist on an orbiting planet's surface. If a rotating planet's distance from its star is small then the star's gravity would cause the planet to stop rotating. This situation is called tidal locking by astronomers.

The result of tidal locking is that one side of the planet always faces its star and the other always faces away from the star. Figure 4.3 illustrates a tidally locked planet orbiting around a red dwarf star. The planet does not rotate.

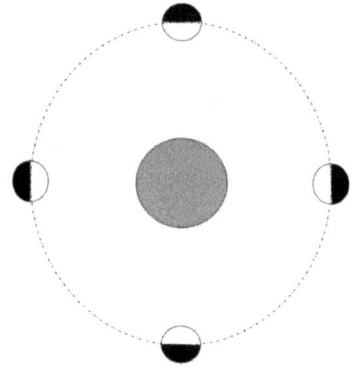

Figure 4.3. Tidally locked planet orbiting a red dwarf.

The side of a tidally locked planet that faced its star would always have daylight while the opposite side would always be in nighttime darkness. The bright side would be hot and the dark side cold.

A second issue with red dwarf stars is that their stellar energy can be variable. According to Wikipedia: "Red dwarfs are often flare stars, which can emit gigantic flares, doubling their brightness in minutes. This variability makes it difficult for life to develop and persist near a red dwarf."[14] The solar flares produced by red dwarfs could strip off an orbiting planet's atmosphere. Both the tidal locking and variable stellar energy could make it extremely difficult if not impossible for the complex life that exists on Earth to evolve on a planet in a red dwarf system.

13. "Red," Habitability, para. 1.
14. "Red," Habitability, para. 2.

Fine-Tuning in Our Solar System

There are also problems with sustaining life on planets in orange dwarf star systems. It has recently been stated that: "new observations show that orange dwarfs emit lots of ultraviolet light long after birth, potentially endangering planetary atmospheres, researchers report."[15] The ultraviolet radiation could destroy an orbiting planet's atmosphere.

As Table 4.1 shows orange and red dwarf stars constitute 88.6 percent of all stars and these stars probably cannot support complex planetary life. Blue giant stars burn out so fast that life would not have time to evolve in their planetary system. We are fortunate that the Earth revolves around a yellow dwarf star, our Sun, which is capable of supporting life on Earth. This is another example of the fine-tuning in our solar system.

Plate tectonics and the related continental drift are also important to sustaining life on Earth. Continental drift involves the movement of massive plates in the Earth's outer rigid shell. According to Ward and Brownlee: "Without plate tectonics, Earth might look much as it did during the first billion and a half years of its existence: a watery world, with only isolated volcanic islands dotting its surface."[16] Plate tectonics result in mountains and continents being formed with dry land on which complex life can evolve.

Shown below in Figure 4.4 is a photo taken in Iceland on the boundary between the North American tectonic plate and the Eurasian tectonic plate.

Figure 4.4. Continental drift in Iceland.

The walking path shown in the photo goes right between the two plates, which are slowly drifting apart by about .8 inches per year. As a result of

15. Crosswell, "'Goldilocks," para. 2.
16. Ward, *Rare*, 194.

this motion the island of Iceland will eventually be split into two parts. One of the plates shown is higher than the other one. It is possible in Iceland to walk from the Eurasian plate to the North American plate and vice versa.

Plate tectonics produce volcanoes that release gases like carbon dioxide into the atmosphere. Carbon dioxide is a greenhouse gas that traps the Sun's energy, and its presence can raise the Earth's temperature. Plate tectonics contribute significantly to the rates and efficiency of what has been called a global thermostat.[17] Plate tectonics also allow for the removal of carbon dioxide, thereby lowering global temperatures, through a reaction with silicate containing minerals resulting from weathering of rocks.

The global thermostat is actually a feedback mechanism, like a home heating system, but on a planetary scale. In a home when the temperature gets too hot the heat turns off; it comes back on when the temperature gets too cold. For the global thermostat carbon dioxide is removed when the Earth gets too hot since the rate of weathering of rocks increases; when the Earth cools less carbon dioxide reacts and is removed, thereby warming the Earth. Thus, plate tectonics helps to regulate the Earth's temperature. The interested reader can check *Rare Earth* for additional details on the global thermostat feedback system.

Within the interior of the Earth, nuclear fission reactions, discussed in chapter 2, take place and they generate heat. The result is that iron in the Earth's core remains molten, and the flow of the molten iron generates a magnetic field around the Earth. This magnetic field is crucial to life because it protects the Earth from damaging cosmic rays.

Wikipedia discusses what cosmic rays are and where they come from:

> Cosmic rays are high-energy particles or clusters of particles (primarily represented by protons or atomic nuclei) that move through space at nearly the speed of light. They originate from the Sun, from outside of the Solar System in our own galaxy, and from distant galaxies.[18]

Without the magnetic field, more dangerous radiation from cosmic rays would reach the Earth's surface and be harmful to life. Also, without a molten core cosmic rays would strip the atmosphere from the Earth, and no complex life would survive. Mars lost its magnetic field and had its atmosphere stripped away a few million years after the planet formed.[19] Plate

17. Ward, *Rare*, 208–12.
18. "Cosmic Rays," para. 2.
19. Gunn, "How."

Fine-Tuning in Our Solar System

tectonics and the Earth's molten iron core are two more examples of fine-tuning in our solar system.

Ward and Brownlee have an interesting chapter[20] discussing why both our Moon and Jupiter are critical to complex life evolving on Earth. There are only three moons revolving around the four inner, rocky planets in our solar system. Mars has two small moons and the Earth has one very large Moon. Our Moon is about one third the size of the Earth and it exerts a strong gravitational force on the Earth.

As illustrated in Figure 4.5, the Earth has an axis of rotation around which it spins. The Moon's gravitational pull on the Earth stabilizes the tilt in the Earth's axis of rotation, so that it stays close to 23.5° from vertical. If this tilt were not stable but varied, then the Earth's axis of rotation would change with time.

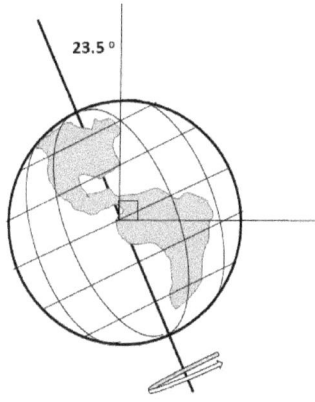

Figure 4.5. Illustration of Earth's axis of rotation.

Figure 4.6 illustrates what would happen over time if we did not have such a large Moon stabilizing the Earth's axis of rotation.

---

20. Ward, *Rare*, chapter 10.

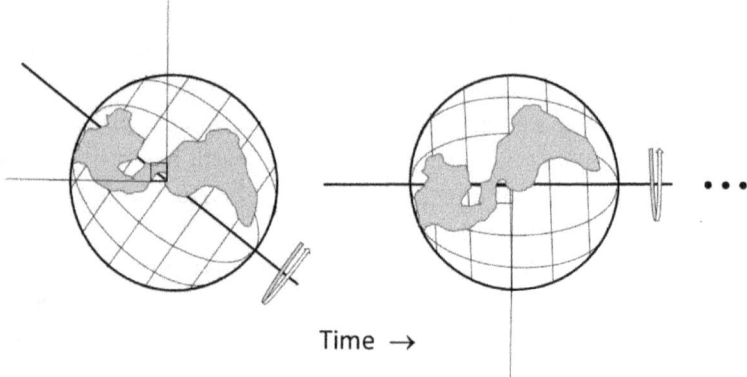

Time →

Figure 4.6. Change in Earth's Axis of Rotation without a Moon over Time.

The result would be that over time the North Pole could migrate down toward the equator, and there would be tremendous changes in climate around the Earth. Areas that were once fertile would become either too cold or too hot for crops to grow. The three dots in Figure 4.6 are there to indicate that the change in the Earth's axis of rotation would be ongoing. Mars has two small moons, but they are too small to stabilize its rotation; hence, Mars's axis of rotation varied widely.

The Moon exerts enough of a gravitational force to increase the Earth's tides, which in turn helps to moderate the Earth's temperature; the tides also help to flush out nutrients from the continents into the oceans and to keep ocean circulation going, which in turn brings thermal energy to higher latitudes and results in more moderate temperatures. Colder temperatures would be more harmful to farming and to most life in these regions.

Now consider Jupiter and how it has helped to protect life on Earth. Figure 4.1A shows how large Jupiter is in relation to Earth. Ward and Brownlee state:

> Jupiter is 318 times more massive than the Earth and it exerts enormous gravitational influence. Its gravitational interactions very efficiently scatter bodies that approach it, and it has largely cleaned out stray bodies from a large volume of the solar system.[21]

About sixty-five million years ago one ten-kilometer-wide body that Jupiter failed to clear hit the Earth. The body was a massive meteorite that

21. Ward, *Rare*, 238.

Fine-Tuning in Our Solar System

struct the Yucatan Peninsula. It has been estimated that this event, called the KT[22] event, resulted in the extinction of 70 percent of the species living on Earth.[23] The effect of the KT event on evolution is discussed in chapter 5. Ward and Brownlee give an estimate that if Jupiter did not exist then the flux of ten-kilometer-wide objects hitting the Earth might be ten thousand times higher.[24] Clearly if this were the case there would be little or no complex life on Earth. So, our large Moon and our large neighbor, Jupiter, are two more examples of fine-tuning in our solar system.

I could go on and give additional details from *Rare Earth*, but I feel that I have made the point. Rather than our solar system being one of billions of solar systems and therefore relatively unimportant, it has some exceptionally unique properties in terms of sustaining life. From the arguments presented in *Rare Earth* one can conclude that only a very, very tiny fraction of stars would have just the right conditions for intelligent life as we know it to exist on a planet revolving around them.

I believe that in the future there is a high probability that primitive life, e.g. bacteria, will be discovered in other parts of the universe. By contrast, I think that it will be much more difficult to find intelligent life in other parts of our universe, but I don't rule out this possibility.

If one considers the information given in this chapter together with the information given in chapter 3 on the fine-tuning of the universe's constants, it seems to me that only two conclusions are logically possible. Either we are the beneficiaries of an extremely large number of unbelievably lucky coincidences, or there is Intelligence behind the creation of the universe as we know it.

The probability of having the physical constants of our universe tuned the way they are is similar to the probability of picking six numbers to win a lottery on a particular day. In addition, the probability of having our own solar system having the properties that is has is similar to the probability of winning the same lottery on the next day. To me it seems essentially impossible that chance led to the creation of our universe with our solar system and the wondrous, finely-tuned laws that govern the universe's physical behavior.

---

22. KT stands for the transition between the Cretaceous and Tertiary periods of geologic time.

23. "KT Event."

24. Ward, *Rare*, 238.

The solar fine-tuning discussed in this chapter gives insight into God's *design imperative*. One goal of the design seems to be to have a limited number of solar systems that could support anthropic life. There is an enormous number of stars in the universe, and many no doubt have planets revolving around them. However, as discussed, our solar system and Earth have many unique, favorable conditions for intelligent life to exist here. These favorable conditions probably only exist on a very, very tiny fraction of planets in our universe.

In chapters 5 to 7 evolution is discussed. Biochemistry in general and proteins in particular are important aspects of evolution. Appendix B gives a brief discussion of proteins for a reader who is not familiar with them. In discussing evolution terms like DNA, enzyme, gene, etc. are defined in the text.

5

Would a Rerun of Evolution Lead to Intelligent Life?

THERE ARE TWO CREATION stories in Genesis and they state that God created humans. The science behind evolution demonstrates that the descriptions in the two stories could not be scientific or historical. Merriam Webster defines evolution as:[1] "the process by which new species or populations of living things develop from preexisting forms through successive generations." Charles Darwin (1809–82) primarily developed the theory of evolution and his research probably created the biggest rift between faith and science of all time. As a result of the rift, evolution is an important subject to reconcile with faith.

Evolution is a difficult subject for non-scientists to understand. Due to its importance the coverage of evolution is split into two parts in which questions raised by two non-believing scientists are discussed. Part 1, discussed in this chapter, addresses the question raised by Stephen Gould who doubted that evolution would lead to intelligent life if it could be rerun.[2] Part 2 in chapter 6 addresses the question raised by Daniel Dennett about

---

1. "Evolution."
2. Gould, *Wonderful*, 14.

whether evolution is purposeless.[3] Although these two questions are different they are also somewhat interrelated.

A different attack on evolution has come from religious people, who proposed Intelligent Design (ID) as an alternative to evolution. The ID people believe Dennett's argument about evolution being purposeless and they propose that God intervened in the evolutionary process to help it along. Chapter 7 discusses why ID is neither correct nor valid science.

In December 1831, Darwin started a voyage around the world on the Beagle, and that trip became an historical milestone. As the ship's naturalist Darwin collected fossils and animal specimens. He visited the Galapagos Islands, where he studied the diversity of life that had developed there in isolation from life on the continent of South America. After his return to England in October 1836, Darwin continued his studies as a naturalist. He published papers and became recognized as a promising young scientist.

In 1859, Darwin published *On the Origin of Species*,[4] describing evolution. In his book Darwin did not address the issue of whether humans themselves evolved. He finally did in 1871, when he published the *Descent of Man*,[5] in which he posits that humans evolved as well and that book created a furor. There are some people who simply cannot bring themselves to accept the logic behind Darwin's theory of evolution and the scientific evidence that backs it up. They do not believe that humans evolved from lower forms of life.

It was during the period after Darwin returned from the Galapagos that the seeds of the theory of evolution began to sprout in his mind. He was influenced by an essay written in 1798 by Thomas Malthus on population dynamics.[6] Malthus pointed out that without disease or starvation, populations can explode out of control. Darwin concluded that these natural forces helped shape the direction of evolution.

By 1844 Darwin had developed the essentials of his theory of evolution, which can be summarized in the following statements:

> First, that all organisms produce more offspring than can possibly survive; second, that all organisms within a species vary, one from the other; third, that at least some of this variation is inherited by offspring. From these three facts we infer the principle of natural

---

3. Dennett, *Darwin's*, 320.
4. Darwin, *Origin*.
5. Darwin, *Descent*.
6. Malthus, *Essay*.

Would a Rerun of Evolution Lead to Intelligent Life?

> selection: since only some of the offspring can survive, on average the survivors will be those variants that, by good fortune, are better adapted to changing local environments. Since these offspring will inherit the favorable variations of their parents, organisms of the next generation will, on average, become better adapted to local conditions.[7]

Since evolution works through generational changes, it is a very slow, gradual process that requires time to achieve its results.

Today we know that it is through genetic transmission that some animals are better adapted for survival than others are. The US National Cancer Institute defines a gene as:[8] "The basic unit of heredity passed from parent to child. Genes are made up of sequences of DNA and are arranged, one after another, at specific locations on chromosomes in the nucleus of cells. They contain information for making specific proteins that lead to the expression of a particular physical characteristic or trait, such as hair color or eye color, or to a particular function in a cell." "Chromosomes are thread-like structures located inside the nucleus of animal and plant cells."[9] Chromosomes are made of proteins and many genes, and humans have a total of forty-six chromosomes, twenty-three from each parent.

The National Library of Medicine describes DNA as:[10] "DNA, or deoxyribonucleic acid, is the hereditary material in humans and almost all other organisms. Nearly every cell in a person's body has the same DNA." The National Library gives the schematic of the double helix DNA shown below in Figure 5.1.

---

7. Zimmer, *Evolution*, xii.
8. "Gene," para. 1.
9. "Chromosomes," para. 1.
10. "What Is DNA," para. 1.

God the Geometer

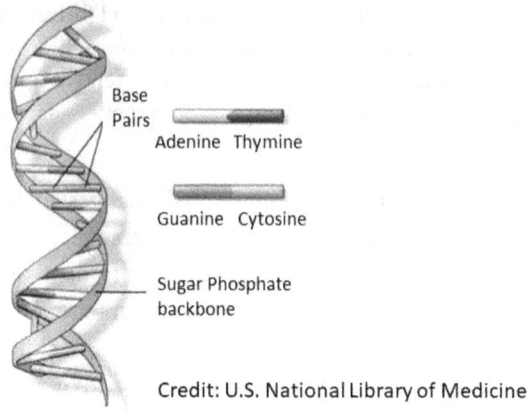

Figure 5.1. Double Helix Structure of DNA.[11]

The National Library of Medicine further states:

> The information in DNA is stored as a code made up of four chemical bases: adenine (A), guanine (G), cytosine (C), and thymine (T). Human DNA consists of about three billion bases, and more than 99 percent of those bases are the same in all people. The order, or sequence, of these bases determines the information available for building and maintaining an organism, similar to the way in which letters of the alphabet appear in a certain order to form words and sentences.[12]

In the case of DNA there are only four letters in its alphabet.

In base pairing, adenine always pairs with thymine, and guanine always pairs with cytosine. Hydrogen bonding holds the base pair molecules together and this type of bonding is weak enough that it can be separated. During replication a section of the DNA molecule is opened by breaking the hydrogen bonds. The process is similar to unzipping a zipper. The open section is then copied, for example to make a protein. The copying process requires several steps and it is described in detail in the free science library Scitable.[13] When cells divide each new cell is given a copy of DNA that matches that in the originating cell.

---

11. "What Is DNA," para. 5.
12. "What Is DNA," para. 2.
13. "Cells."

Would a Rerun of Evolution Lead to Intelligent Life?

Sometimes errors can occur when DNA is copied during cell division. This change in a genetic sequence is called a genetic mutation. Genetic mutations can be caused by copying errors, radiation, chemicals, or infectious agents. Darwin was not aware of genes and he did not know what we know today about genes, but his theory of evolution predicted the outcomes that genetic transmission leads to.

When a genetic mutation occurs, it can either be beneficial or disadvantageous. For example, some genetic mutations can lead to cancer. A beneficial mutation will enhance one's ability to survive and as a result it will be passed on to the next generation. It is through this process of passing on desirable traits that evolution leads to change. However, in some cases no mutations occur when genes are copied; in other cases, a harmful mutation that does not enhance survivability occurs; lastly a beneficial mutation can be passed on. As a result, it can take some time before a beneficial mutation is passed on, and evolution moves forward.

Assume that evolution takes place on a planet revolving around a star. In order to allow time for evolutionary change to take place, its star has to burn and supply energy to the planet for a very long time. As mentioned earlier, our Sun has burned for about 4.5 million years and it is probably halfway through its life. The long life of our Sun perfectively matches the long timescale required for evolution to take place on Earth.

Although many people cannot accept the fact that humans evolved from lower mammals, I do not think that this issue is a key one in terms of the challenge that evolution poses to faith. In my opinion, there are two key issues. One key issue is the claim that if the clock could be set back and evolution rerun, then intelligent life, *Homo sapiens*, would not result. Stephen Gould raised this issue when he said: "Wind back the tape of life to the early days of the Burgess Shale; let it play again from an identical starting point, and the chance becomes vanishingly small that anything like human intelligence would grace the replay."[14]

In *Finding Darwin's God*, Kenneth Miller quotes one of Gould's students, Kurt Wise, on his mentor's position:

> To conclude, as Gould does, that man is a wildly improbable evolutionary event, a detail, not a purpose, and a cosmic accident is disconcerting to some, but not to Gould. To him, release from any purpose is 'exhilarating' as it also releases any responsibility to

---

14. Gould, *Wonderful*, 14.

any other, offering maximum freedom to thrive, or to fail, in our chosen way.[15]

Both Wise and Miller disagree with Gould's position. Miller states Wise's position about where he feels the real danger of evolutionary biology could lie: "It is the chilling prospect that evolution might succeed in convincing humanity of the fundamental purposelessness of life. Without purpose to the universe, there is no meaning, there are no absolutes, and there is no reason for existence." Wise's comments on purposelessness directly address the comments made by Daniel Dennett,[16] when he claimed that evolution is a purposeless process.

In examining evolution, I believe that one has to do so in a clear-eyed, fair, and objective manner. In this regard I agree with Dennett when he describes the effect that such an examination might produce:

> What if it turns out that the sweet vision—or a better one—survives intact, strengthened and deepened by the encounter? Wouldn't it be a shame to forgo the opportunity for a strengthened, renewed creed, settling instead for a fragile, sickbed faith that you mistakenly supposed must not be disturbed?[17]

I would like to try to carry out a clear-eyed evaluation of evolution and let the chips fall where they may.

Dan Kuebler has presented a really excellent and thorough article[18] on order, chance, and design in evolution.[19] In the article Kuebler gives concrete facts that refute Gould's argument that a rerun of evolution would lead to a different outcome. Kuebler begins by pointing out the difference between random and chance events. A random event cannot be predicted, whereas a chance event has some probability of occurrence. Evolution definitely has some order built in and it is not a random process, but evolution can be affected by chance events.

One example of a chance event affecting evolution that Kuebler gives, involves the extinction of dinosaurs that occurred sixty-five million years ago, which is called the KT event. The KT event, discussed in chapter 4,

15. Miller, *Finding*, 187.
16. Dennett, *Darwin's*, 320.
17. Dennett, *Darwin's*, 22.
18. Kuebler, "Order."

19. It is interesting that Kuebler's article appeared on the website purposefuluniverse.com, whose title is the exact opposite of what Dennett has proposed about our universe.

Would a Rerun of Evolution Lead to Intelligent Life?

involved a large meteorite striking the Earth. Thanks to Jupiter, very large meteorites have rarely hit the Earth in the past but there is a finite probability the Earth could be hit again. During the KT event, the meteorite drastically changed the Earth's climate, resulting the extinction of all dinosaurs except for birds. Small mammals survived the meteorite impact and humans have evolved from these survivors.

As an example of the order in evolution, Kuebler considers a cell's genome. The genome is the entire set of DNA instructions found in a cell. Kuebler points out that:

> mutations do not occur with equal likelihood throughout an organism's genome. In fact, there are regions known as mutational hotspots in which mutations are much more likely to occur. There are environmental stresses that increase the likelihood of mutations occurring in specific regions of an organism's genome. This process is the opposite of random; it is evolutionarily adaptive for the organism.[20]

Another example of order in evolution that Kuebler gives, involves protein folding. Proteins become biologically active when they are folded correctly into three dimensional shapes. Kuebler states:

> Despite the existence of a nearly infinite array of possible amino acid sequences, proteins predominately fold into two distinct secondary structures, beta-sheets and alpha helices." He further states: "These [2] forms are not 'built by the evolutionary process' but are rather dictated by physical and chemical constraints. If evolution were to run again, beta-sheet and alpha helices would certainly form any time amino acids are strung together in a chain.[21]

Kuebler references paleontologist Simon Conway Morris' book, *Life's Solution*,[22] and states: "that there is an underlying order that funnels evolution, and that, regardless of the exact pattern of mutations, this order allows evolution to converge upon certain robust forms."[23] This process is referred to as convergent evolution and "flight is a classic example, as flying insects, birds, pterosaurs, and bats have independently evolved the useful capacity of flight."[24] Indeed, in *Life's Solution* Conway devotes chapters 6 to 10 to

20. Kuebler, "Order," 4.
21. Kuebler, "Order," 12.
22. Morris, *Life's Solution*.
23. Kuebler, "Order," 14.
24. "Convergent," para. 1.

discussing the numerous examples of evolutionary convergence that have occurred.

Kuebler gives the example of convergence involving endothermy, the process of regulating body temperature through metabolism, when he states:

> Another key mammalian trait, endothermy has evolved multiple times in mammals, birds, fish and insects. The point of this is that the mammalian traits were not a one-time occurrence evolutionarily. Rerun evolution again and you are likely to get creatures with these traits. While the pattern and timing of the emergence of these traits would be different each time due to the contingent [chance] nature of evolution, these solutions are such a good way of "making a living" on our planet that they would appear again.[25]

Lastly, Kuebler discusses why dinosaurs had some characteristics that were inferior to those of mammals. He states:

> For example, the fact that dinosaurs laid eggs made their offspring particularly vulnerable to environmental changes (it also is one factor that allowed them to evolve to such enormous sizes). On the other hand, the fact that mammals give birth to live young and invest more resources in nourishing their offspring likely gave mammals a greater chance of surviving in an ever-changing environment (although this reproductive style limits body size).[26]

So even if the KT event never occurred mammals had characteristics that would have led to their being the dominant species on the Earth.

Based on Kuebler's insightful analysis whether a rerun of evolution would lead to intelligent life is not a question of if but when. Had the KT event not occurred the results of evolution would be the same but the timing would be different.

In the beginning of this chapter it was pointed out that evolution through natural selection leads to species that have improved survival capabilities. The survival capabilities of humans are truly astounding. If one examines what humans have achieved in countless areas such as medicine, science, engineering, housing, and farming, to name a few, the results are staggering.

We have been able to place a man on the Moon. We have cured many diseases and have greatly extended the average lifetimes of humans. We

25. Kuebler, "Order," 16–17.
26. Kuebler, "Order," 15.

Would a Rerun of Evolution Lead to Intelligent Life?

have advanced our scientific knowledge to the point where we can understand the Big Bang and evolution, as well as the implications of each. Today, people are warning about the over use of antibiotics because of the way that bacteria can evolve and mutate, become resistant to drugs, and defeat the purpose of the medicines. Other animals simply don't begin to come close to *Homo sapiens* in terms of their survival capabilities. In short, humans have powers for surviving that absolutely dwarf those of any other species.

The key reason for our overwhelming success at surviving is our superior intellect. Consider the question of rerunning evolution. Given what intelligent life has achieved on Earth, why would evolution not progress toward intelligent life again? Simply stating that a rerun of evolution would not lead to intelligent life is not enough without giving concrete facts to back up the statement.

For the counter argument, Kuebler has presented many scientific facts that support his position that there is an underlying order in evolution, even though chance plays a role. Evolution is definitely not a random process. As Kenneth Miller puts it:

> And, to ask the big question, do we have to assume that from the beginning He planned intelligence and consciousness to develop in a bunch of nearly hairless, bipedal, African primates? If another group of animals had evolved to self-awareness, if another creature had shown itself worthy of a soul, can we really say for certain that God would have been less pleased with His new Adam and Eve? I don't think so.[27]

Examining whether a rerun of evolution would lead to intelligent life leads to the following insight into God's *design imperative*. Evolution indicates that there is true freedom built into the design of our universe. Genetic mutations lead to enhanced survivability, but they can also lead to problems such as cancer. Chapters 8 and 9 discuss in more detail the freedom that we experience in our universe. Putting it succinctly, true freedom requires something to be free about. If we lived in a world that was designed to be perfect from the start, i.e. had no natural evils such as disease, earthquakes, severe storms, etc., how would be able to express our freedom? There would be nothing to be free about.

---

27. Miller, *Finding*, 274.

6

What Is the Purpose of Evolution?

In his book *Darwin's Dangerous Idea* Daniel Dennett states: "Evolution is a mindless, purposeless, algorithmic process."[1] An algorithm is a set of rules to be followed to solve a problem, typically using a computer. An example of an algorithm is given below. If Dennett is correct, then a paradox exists involving the theories of the Big Bang and evolution, and I don't see how this paradox can reasonably be explained. As discussed in chapters 2 to 4, the Big Bang and the tuning of the cosmic and solar system parameters almost certainly point toward the development of life and a Creator of our universe. There appears to be a definite purpose and direction to the Big Bang, namely life, especially intelligent life, as we know it. Once life starts, if evolution points nowhere then the combination of the Big Bang followed by evolution is more than strange.

Did a Creator design the universe for life and then stop there and let purposelessness take over? Or, is there a purpose and direction to evolution that can be discerned?

Dennett has an excellent section in *Darwin's Dangerous Idea*[2] that discusses processes, such as evolution, as algorithms. According to Dennett, an algorithm possesses the three key characteristics:

1. Dennett, *Darwin's*, 320.
2. Dennett, *Darwin's*, 48–60.

1. *Substrate neutrality:* The procedure works equally well with pencil or pen, paper or parchment, neon light, or skywriting, using any symbol system you like.
2. *Underlying mindlessness:* No thinking is involved. One only has to follow fixed rules.
3. *Guaranteed results:* The algorithm always gives an answer if executed correctly.

As an example of an algorithm, Dennett discusses long division. His particular example involves the following problem: How many times does 47 go into 326,574? Or:

$$47 \overline{) 326574}^{\,?}$$

Only a whole number is sought for an answer.[3]

An algorithm to solve the problem is as follows. First, guess a digit between 0 and 9 at random, and multiply this digit by 47. Subtract the result from 326 to give a remainder,[4] and if this remainder is greater than 46 then increase the initial guess by 1 and start over. If the remainder is a negative number, decrease the initial guess by 1 and start over. If the remainder is between 0 and 46, then keep the digit in the answer and append to the remainder all the digits in the dividend that were not used, namely 574. This new number, remainder with 574 appended, is used as the dividend, and the process of choosing a random digit is repeated using the highest three digits of the new dividend. The next digit that results from the repetition of the algorithm is appended to the answer. The process stops when the dividend is a number between 0 and 46.

Clearly this algorithm is substrate neutral; it does not depend on how the calculations are carried out. Even though it might be difficult to teach a child long division, the algorithm is mindless. The rules for the algorithm can be blindly followed without the person's doing any thinking to work out the logic behind them. Finally, the long division algorithm is guaranteed to

---

3. An algorithm to generate an answer with a fractional component could easily be written. For brevity digits to the right of the decimal point are not considered in this descriptive example.

4. The algorithm could be written so that the 3-digit number chosen, 326, was part of the algorithmic process. The initial part of the dividend chosen has to be in the range of 0 to 9 times 47. For brevity the use of the first 3 digits of the dividend is simply assumed.

converge to an answer, namely how many times does 47 go into 326,574 excluding any decimal result, called the quotient. This is the objective of the algorithm.

Algorithms are used all the time in computer calculations, which take advantage of the fact that they can be represented as a set of blind rules, and when they are properly executed they produce an answer. The speed of computers results in algorithms being extremely useful calculation tools. Although an algorithm is mindless, that does not mean that evolution, which is algorithmic, is purposeless.

Mindless and purposeless are not the same. In Dennett's division example there is a definite purpose to the algorithm, which is to find the largest integer number that the dividend, 326,574, is divisible by the divisor, 47. So, the mindless division algorithm has a purpose, and indeed every algorithm has a purpose. The major problem with Dennett's discussion of evolution is not that it is algorithmic, but his contention that evolution is purposeless.

Now consider one type of computer algorithm that has been used to solve mathematical optimization problems. This type of algorithm is called a genetic algorithm, and it is modelled after evolution itself. Computer-based genetic algorithms have been used to solve complex mathematical optimization problems.

Assume that one has a mathematical description of the profit obtained by selling a product, and that the profit depends on many variables, called independent variables. In optimizing profit, one wants to find the very best solution (set of independent variables), called the global optimum, since it gives the maximum possible profit. One can use computer-based genetic algorithms to solve for the independent variables that maximize profit. One of the most important attributes of computer-based genetic algorithms is that they are able to deal with problems that have many different optimum values.

Consider the topographical plot shown in Figure 6.1 in which there are three peaks, A, B, and C.

What Is the Purpose of Evolution?

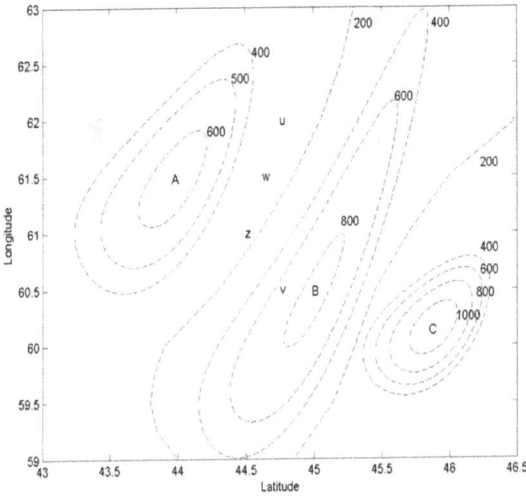

Figure 6.1. Topographical map showing peaks.

Contours of constant height are shown for each peak. Peak C is the highest and therefor the global optimum. The other two peaks are local optima, since they only have the maximum height in their own neighborhood. Many computer-based optimization algorithms have been proposed that can be used to find the peaks using a mathematical model of the topology, but some of them would only find a local optimum such as peaks A or B. Genetic algorithms are capable of finding the very best solution possible to a particular optimization problem, namely the global optimum.

Although they only use local information, genetic algorithms are able to get across valleys and find the peak with the maximum height. Genetic algorithms do not get stuck at local optima, as other algorithms can. Genetic algorithms start with using local information, since that is how biological evolution works.

For example, Darwin found that finches on different islands in the Galapagos had different attributes, depending on the type of food available on an island. Darwin's research journal included the illustration, shown in Figure 6.2, of four finches from four different Galapagos Islands.

God the Geometer

Figure 6.2. Specialized finch beaks noted by Darwin.[5]

As can be seen, the finches' beaks are specialized for their diet on the island they inhabit, be it hard seeds, insects, or other food.

It is difficult to give a simple description of how genetic optimization algorithms work, and how they expand their local information to find a global optimum. As a result, a discussion is included in Appendix C showing how they could be used to solve the topology optimization problem illustrated in Figure 6.1. The genetic algorithm described there incorporates the essence of the algorithmic processes that occur in biological evolution. As a result, its attributes and those of evolution are the same.

In 1864 Herbert Spencer coined the phrase survival of the fittest in reference to evolution in his *Principles of Biology*.[6] Evolution strives to find the global optimum for the problem of survival, just as the genetic optimization algorithm, discussed above, tries to find the globally highest peak. The word "fittest" in survival of the fittest indicates the optimization nature of the evolution algorithm. In Darwinian terms the phrase is best understood as: "survival of the form that will leave the most copies of itself

---

5. "Galapagos."
6. Spencer, *Principles*, 444.

What Is the Purpose of Evolution?

in successive generations."[7] The word most in the preceding sentence indicates the optimization-based nature of evolution.

Each new product of natural selection is superior in terms of survivability to its predecessors; otherwise it would not have evolved. Evolution's purpose is optimization-based, and since it has a purpose it has a direction, namely toward maximum survivability. As long as a rich pattern of inheritance and mutations is explored and enough time is given for the search, evolution will eventually find the global optimum.

Now consider what the global optimum of survival of the fittest involves. In the one case on Earth where the evolution algorithm has been run, the result is *Homo sapiens*. In terms of survival of the fittest, *Homo sapiens* has capabilities that are orders and orders of magnitude superior to those of any other animal life form. *Homo sapiens* corresponds to a mountain peak that has the height of Mount Everest, while the other peaks in the survival problem are tiny hills. In chapter 5 the accomplishments of humans in areas such as medicine, engineering, housing, farming, and understanding science are pointed out. Since 1900 the global average life expectancy of humans has more than doubled and is now above seventy years.[8] No other animal comes anywhere close to humans in terms of achieving such an increase in survivability.

Now consider the question of re-running evolution that was considered in chapter 5. If evolution is a good algorithm, why would it not find the same global optimum again? The peak that involves intelligent life is orders and orders of magnitude higher than that for any other animal life form on Earth. The fact that evolution is a good algorithm can be discerned from the vast diversity of life that existed in the past and that exists today. In trying to optimize survival, evolution has produced countless species over the millennia. Species that became extinct could not compete or adapt to change as well as the survivors could.

When people think of survival of the fittest, the image that probably comes to mind is something like a pack of lions ripping apart a helpless victim. In *The Selfish Gene*, Richard Dawkins describes his view of evolution by quoting Tennyson's famous phrase: "I think 'nature red in the tooth and claw' sums up our modern understanding of natural selection admirably."[9]

---

7. "Survival," para. 1.
8. Rosner, "Life," para. 4.
9. Dawkins, *Selfish*, 2.

God the Geometer

In the case of hominids, however, survival of the fittest takes on a deeper meaning. Hominids lacked the natural weapons of some of the animals that were likely to prey on them. Hominids include modern humans, *Homo sapiens*, as well as chimpanzees, and orangutans plus all their immediate ancestors. They did not have great strength, great speed, powerful jaws, or claws with which to defend themselves like for example lions. What they developed was superior brain power, and this development no doubt led to early hominids banding together in groups.

Hominids evolved into a supremely social species. Groups of hominids could hunt together and provide mutual defense. As social interaction grew, the behavior patterns of hominids changed and became more complex.

The description provided by Zimmer, paraphrasing Andrew Whitten, a Scottish primatologist, nicely sums up the evolutionary process that probably occurred:

> Hominid evolution may have become a feedback loop of ever-increasing social intelligence, producing our ever-expanding brains. Ultimately, this evolutionary spiral transformed hominid society itself. It eventually became too hard for a dominant male to enforce a hierarchy in his band because his subordinates had become too clever. Hominid society shifted from a chimp like hierarchy to an egalitarian structure. Only when hominids began to live in an egalitarian society, Whiten argues, could they finally take advantage of the hunter gatherer way of life. Men could work together to plan a hunt, and they could leave the women and children behind without being paralyzed by suspicion. Likewise, women could organize expeditions of their own to find tubers[10] and other plants. With tools and cooperation, hominids carved themselves a new ecological niche in the savanna.[11]

In the case of *Homo sapiens*, however, survival of the fittest takes on a more profound meaning. No longer was an overt "nature red in tooth and claw" approach the optimum approach to survival. Although such an approach lays at the root of many of the behavior patterns of humans, it can be superseded. Richard Dawkins has a very interesting chapter in his book *The Selfish Gene* entitled:[12] "Nice Guys Finish First." In it he describes

---

10. An enlarged, fleshy, reproductive, and food storage structure produced on an underground stem (a potato is a tuber).
11. Zimmer, *Evolution*, 272.
12. Dawkins, *Selfish*, chap. 12.

What Is the Purpose of Evolution?

why cooperation, and not confrontation, makes sense in addressing certain types of conflicts within a group. Cooperation between individuals can be labeled altruistic behavior.

In commenting on Dawkins' book, Kenneth Miller states:

> Darwinian evolution can produce cooperation and care just as surely as conflict and competition. The care and self-sacrifice seen in animal families are not an exception to evolution rather they are the straightforward results of natural selection acting to favor instinctive altruism. Under the right circumstances, nice guys really do finish first. Once again, Darwin got it right.[13]

Michael Ruse, a philosopher and author of *Can A Darwinian Be A Christian*, distinguishes between instinctive or biological altruism and true or moral altruism.[14] Biological altruism is done with the expectation of an evolutionary return to the giver. For example, caring for one's offspring insures the propagation of the caregiver's genes. Biological altruism is similar to the idea that I'll scratch your back if you scratch mine. True altruism is done for the good of other individuals, and without the expectation of any reward.

Ruse speculates that evolution tries to make us good biological altruists by using natural selection to make us good moral altruists:

> We are social animals, we need something. . .to make us interact with our fellow humans, to make us biological altruists. And this something is going to be the moral urge: the feeling that we 'ought' to do certain things, even though our nature is against it.[15]

My initial reaction to Ruse's statement was that it seemed backwards. I would have thought that biological altruism would come first, followed by moral altruism. I posed this question to Ruse, who told me that the majority of sociobiologists would agree with his ordering that puts moral altruism first. He pointed out that when we developed intelligence we also developed moral altruism. Another name I would use for moral altruism is conscience.[16]

Today many people have a deep-seated inner sense about doing good for others. I think that most people have felt the urge to do something

---

13. Miller, *Finding*, 248.
14. Ruse, *Can*.
15. Ruse, *Can*, 195.
16. Ruse, "Personal."

simply because it is the right thing to do. Even Richard Dawkins, who is a proponent of the strong influence that genes exert on all behavior, has some very interesting comments on true altruism: "It is possible that yet another unique quality of man is a capacity for genuine, disinterested, true altruism. I hope so, but I am not going to argue the case one way or another."[17]

The capacity to be concerned about others is something that many theists, agnostics, and atheists seem to share. Comparing believers and non-believers, Dennett, who is a non-believer, states: "What both groups share, in spite of their differences in their deepest creeds, is a conviction that life does have meaning, that goodness matters."[18]

Also, Dawkins states:

> Let us try to teach generosity and altruism, because we are born selfish. Let us understand what our own selfish genes are up to, because we may then at least have the chance to upset their designs, something that no other species has ever aspired to.[19]

Clearly Dawkins feels that humans have the potential to control their genetic impulses. Our behavior, though influenced by our genes, is not one hundred percent hard wired in. There are occasions where people do good for others because they feel deep down inside that it is the right thing to do, and not because they will be rewarded for their actions.

Evolution through natural selection and survival of the fittest leads in the direction of human beings expressing true altruism towards others. However, the ultimate achievement of true altruism does not come from evolution, but rather through spiritual power arising from our spiritual souls.

Further, it is interesting to examine just what survival means. To us as individuals, survival means living a long, happy, productive, and healthy life. We also want to see our offspring lead similar lives as well.

To Dawkins, all life forms, plant and animal, are simply survival machines that house genes.[20] The survival machines, including humans, are manipulated by genes so that the genes themselves can become immortal. A gene tries to become immortal by surviving through as many generations of survival machines as possible. Thus, within life as we know it, there is the

---

17. Dawkins, *Selfish*, 200.
18. Dennett, *Darwin's*, 18.
19. Dawkins, *Selfish*, 3.
20. Dawkins, *Selfish*, 24.

What Is the Purpose of Evolution?

very strong tendency toward survival, whether we look at humans, at other animals, or at genes.

Since optimizing survivability is the objective of evolution, this survival tendency is not at all surprising. Yet physical survival is doomed to failure. People die, and even if their genes survive for many generations, the universe has a finite amount of energy and it will eventually end along with all the genes. So even though we have a built-in biological drive for survival, its physical attainment is ultimately impossible.

Now consider what many religions promise, namely eternal life. This adds a totally new dimension to the survival picture. Since I am a Christian I will speak from this perspective. Christ has promised that we as unique individuals can live forever. Because of our evolutionary predisposition toward survival, eternal life is a concept that should resonate throughout our entire being. We are genetically predisposed to survival, and we should be energized to do whatever it takes to achieve the reward of eternal life.

Christ taught us that the way to achieve eternal life is straightforward. The following dialog took place when Jesus was questioned on what needed to be done to achieve eternal life:

> Then an expert on the law stood up to test Jesus, saying, "Teacher, what must I do to get life forever?" Jesus said, "What is written in the law? What do you read there?" The man answered, "Love the Lord your God with all your heart, all your soul, all your strength, and all your mind." Also, "Love your neighbor as you love yourself." Jesus said to him, "Your answer is right. Do this and you will live"(Luke 10:25–28).

Loving our neighbor as ourselves is simply expressing true altruism toward our neighbor. The two commandments in the law come from the Old Testament; to love God comes from "Love the Lord your God with all your heart, all your soul, and all your strength" (Deut 5:6), and to love one's neighbor comes from, "Forget about the wrong things people do to you, and do not try to get even. Love your neighbor as you love yourself. I am the Lord" (Lev 19:18).

The expert on the law followed up his first question to Jesus with another:

> But the man, wanting to show the importance of his question, said to Jesus, "And who is my neighbor?" Jesus answered, "As a man was going down from Jerusalem to Jericho, some robbers attacked him. They tore off his clothes, beat him, and left him lying there,

almost dead. It happened that a priest was going down that road. When he saw the man, he walked by on the other side. Next, a Levite came there, and after he went over and looked at the man, he walked by on the other side of the road. Then a Samaritan traveling down the road came to where the hurt man was. When he saw the man, he felt very sorry for him. The Samaritan went to him, poured olive oil and wine on his wounds, and bandaged them. Then he put the hurt man on his own donkey and took him to an inn where he cared for him. The next day, the Samaritan brought out two coins, gave them to the innkeeper, and said, 'Take care of this man. If you spend more money on him, I will pay it back to you when I come again.'" Then Jesus said, "Which one of these three men do you think was a neighbor to the man who was attacked by the robbers?" The expert on the law answered, "The one who showed him mercy." Jesus said to him, "Then go and do what he did." (Luke 10: 29–37).

What makes this story particularly poignant is the relationship that existed between the Jews and the Samaritans. The Samaritans practiced a religion closely related to Judaism but they were not accepted by the Jews, and the Jews and Samaritans did not like one another. Only the Samaritan pays attention to this poor victim and takes the time to help him out. We are encouraged to do likewise for our fellow man.

Christian morality goes much deeper than the morality one might expect from evolution, but the altruism resulting from evolution is certainly something that is totally harmonious with Christianity. It is interesting that a few centuries after Christ lived, Christianity was thriving while Rome had collapsed. Rome with its coliseum games in which gladiators fought brutally to the death and Christians were thrown to lions embodied nature red in the tooth and claw. Yet Christianity outlived Rome!

True altruism, one of the tendencies produced by our evolutionary breeding, is precisely what loving our neighbor is all about. Clearly, evolution has also produced a selfish side to humans as well, and this side needs to be controlled. However, what evolution has achieved in shaping human nature gives us some of the attributes that are necessary to achieve eternal life. We can use our intellect to discover God through his revelation and his creation, involving such things as the Big Bang, our solar system, and evolution.

There is no conflict between evolution and faith; rather, evolution predisposes humans to appreciate the message and ultimate objective of

What Is the Purpose of Evolution?

eternal life espoused by many religions. So, when Dennett says that evolution is a purposeless algorithm he is completely wrong as is Gould when he says a rerun of evolution would not lead to intelligent life.

Examining whether evolution has a purpose gives insight into another aspect of God's *design imperative* for our universe. Evolution's purpose of maximizing survivability can lead humans toward true altruism in their dealings with others. True altruism in turn prepares humans for the message that many faiths profess that there is life after death, i.e. the ability to have infinite survivability. Thus, evolution is not antagonistic toward faith but rather it provides a basis for increased faith.

A second insight into God's *design imperative* comes from the order that is built into evolution, which was discussed in chapter 5. The order involved in the fine-tuning of our universe's physical constants and our solar system is matched by the order that convergence indicates takes place in evolution. While chance plays a definite role, the design of evolution definitely is not random. The convergent aspects of evolution coupled with the superior aspects of the evolutionary algorithm, indicate that if it were rerun, intelligent life would emerge again.

7

Why Intelligent Design Is Not Valid Science

THE DEVELOPMENT OF THE term Intelligent Design (ID) has an interesting history. ID arose as an extension of attempts to counter the scientific arguments that are the basis for the theory of evolution. In 1925 the famous Scopes Monkey trial was held in Tennessee. John Scopes, a high school teacher, was convicted of violating Tennessee's 1925 Butler Act, which prohibited the teaching of "any theory that denies the Story of Divine Creation of Man as taught in the Bible, and to teach instead that man has descended from a lower order of animal."[1] Scopes was convicted but the conviction was thrown out on a technicality and the decision was never challenged.

In the 1920s the following states also passed anti-evolution laws: Florida, Oklahoma, Arkansas, and Mississippi. Tennessee's Butler Act was rescinded in 1967, and the Supreme Court upheld the right to teach evolution in 1968.

Since science was winning in the courts, evolution opponents decided to emphasize science in their position. As a result, the term scientific creationism was coined. Proponents of scientific creationism claimed that the Earth was only a few thousand years old and that all species were created after a great world flood. In addition to having religious underpinnings, both claims were easily shown to be scientifically incorrect.

---

1. Coyne, "Case," para. 7.

Why Intelligent Design Is Not Valid Science

Coyne has an extensive discussion on the history of lawsuits associated with scientific creationism and ID. Coyne states: "In 1981, the Arkansas legislature passed an 'equal time' bill mandating balanced treatment for 'evolution science' and 'creation science' in the classroom."[2] The bill was challenged in the courts and ruled to be unconstitutional, since it involved among other things the government advancing religion. In 1986 a similar law in Louisiana was also ruled to be unconstitutional by the US Supreme Court (Edwards vs Aguillard). The decision outlawed teaching creation science in public schools.

The creationists then came up with the phrase intelligent design (ID). *Of Pandas and People*[3] was a creationist textbook that was aimed at high school biology classes and it was the first place where the phrase ID was used. Once the Edwards vs. Aguillard decision came down, all references to creation science were replaced in the book with the phrase ID.[4] The first edition of *Of Pandas and People* was published in 1989 and the second edition in 1993. In the second edition a chapter on blood clotting was contributed by Michael Behe. Behe's hypothesis of blood clotting supporting ID is discussed in detail below.

The teaching of ID was challenged in a 2005 Pennsylvania trial, and a federal district court issued a ruling about teaching ID. The ruling stated: "ID was not science, that it 'cannot uncouple itself from its creationist, and thus religious, antecedents,' and that the public school district's promotion of it therefore violated the Establishment Clause of the First Amendment to the United States Constitution."[5] So, at present it is unconstitutional to teach ID in public schools.

Wikipedia has an extensive web page on ID[6] that correctly points out that ID is a pseudoscience that does not make any testable predictions about our universe, and therefore it is not science. The Intelligent Design Network, a proponent of ID, has on its website the following statement:

> ID holds that certain features of the universe and of living things are best explained by an intelligent cause rather than an undirected process such as natural selection. ID is thus a scientific disagreement with the core claim of evolutionary theory that the apparent

---

2. Coyne, "Case," para. 11.
3. Thaxton, *Pandas*.
4. "Intelligent Design," para. 2.
5. "Intelligent Design," para. 2.
6. "Intelligent Design."

design of living systems is an illusion that can be adequately explained by only the natural sorting of random mutations.[7]

There are two problems with the Intelligent Design Network's statement. First, as explained in chapter 6 evolution has a purpose, namely maximum survivability. Thus, it is incorrect to say evolution is undirected. Second, as discussed in chapter 5 chance events can affect evolution but chance events are not random as stated. From the statement by the Intelligent Design Network one can conclude that they definitely agree with Dennett's statement, refuted in chapter 6, that evolution is purposeless.[8]

Wikipedia also points out: "ID presents two main arguments against evolutionary explanations: irreducible complexity and specified complexity, asserting that certain biological and informational features of living things are too complex to be the result of natural selection."[9] This chapter discusses and points out the flaws in irreducible complexity. Excellent arguments have also been given to refute specified complexity. Neither type of complexity is scientific and neither is valid.

Michael Behe, who is a biochemist and a Professor of Biological Sciences at Lehigh University, is the best-known advocate for irreducible complexity. Behe seized upon Darwin's statement that if evolution works, complex systems can only be formed by many gradual modifications. Evolution does not allow a sudden jump directly to a complex system.

Lee Strobel, who believes in ID, wrote *The Case For A Creator*, and he interviewed Behe for his book. In the interview Behe discusses what he calls the concept of irreducible complexity:

> You see, a system or device is irreducibly complex if it has a number of different components that all work together to accomplish the task of the system, and if you were to remove one of the components, the system would no longer function. An irreducibly complex system is highly unlikely to be built piece by piece through Darwinian processes, because the system has to be fully present in order for it to function.[10]

A simple non-biological example of irreducible complexity that Behe used to make his point is a mouse trap and one is shown in Figure 7.1.

7. "Intelligent Design/Teleology," para. 2.
8. Dennett, *Darwin's*, 320.
9. "Intelligent Design," para. 3.
10. Strobel, *Case*, 19.

Why Intelligent Design Is Not Valid Science

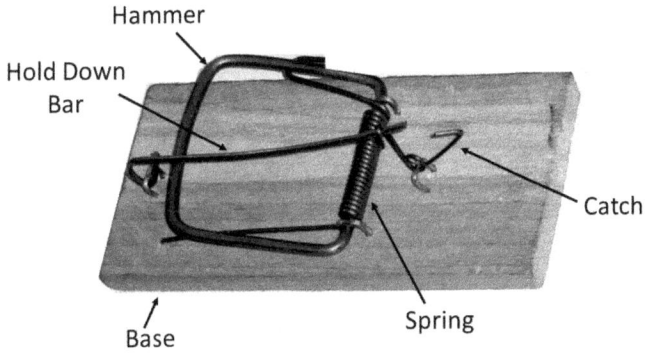

Figure 7.1. Mouse trap.[11]

The trap has five parts, a base, catch, spring, hold down bar, and hammer. Behe contends that if any part is removed then the trap will not work, and thus, it is irreducibly complex.

To refute Behe, John MacDonald published a paper entitled: A Reducibly Complex Mousetrap.[12] MacDonald shows five different mousetrap designs of increasing complexity, and his paper has animations to show how each design would work. The five designs use the five parts identified by Behe, and each design adds one part to the preceding design. Each design is an improvement over the preceding design that results from adding one new part. MacDonald points out that a trap with five parts is more efficient than one with a single part. However, what is important is that a one-part trap could still work even if it is not particularly efficient.

Kenneth Miller, in addition to discussing MacDonald's trap sequence, points out that: "Behe argues that natural selection cannot favor the evolution of a non-functional system (which is true), and then argues that no portion of an 'irreducibly complex' system (such as a mousetrap) could have any function."[13] However, Miller points out a flaw in Behe's argument, which is that he can use three of the mouse trap parts to make a tie clip. He simply removes the hold down bar and the catch. So, these three parts of a mousetrap could be used for another function, contrary to what Behe says.

---

11. "Mouse."
12. McDonald, "Reducibly."
13. Miller, "Mousetrap."

In many cases evolution repurposes an existing component for a different function. Repurposing is one mechanism for building up an irreducibly complex system from smaller, pre-existing components. In nature evolution would typically add only one new component to an existing system, not the two that would be required for Miller's tie clip. However, Miller's tie clip example exposes a major flaw with Behe's irreducible complexity hypothesis.

In his interview with Strobel, Behe describes three biological systems that he claims are irreducibly complex. The first involves cilia, minute hair like organelles, on the surface of cells; the second involves cells that have a flagellum, which is a whip like appendage that produces cell motion; and the third involves the blood clotting cascade. In *Finding Darwin's God*,[14] Kenneth Miller addresses all three of these examples, and he also presents additional evidence against the claim of irreducible complexity.

I want to focus only on the blood clotting example. The interested reader is referred to Miller's book for a complete exposition of his arguments against irreducible complexity. Blood clotting is a complicated biochemical process that involves many sequential steps. Assume that a cut triggers the production of a small amount of an enzyme, called a clotting factor. An enzyme is a protein that increases the rate of a chemical reaction without itself undergoing any permanent chemical change. This process is called catalysis.

One molecule of the initial clotting factor catalyzes the production of a great many molecules of a second clotting factor. The second clotting factor, another enzyme, proceeds to catalyze the formation of many more molecules of the next clotting factor. This process continues through a number of such steps. Thus, blood clotting involves amplification through an enzyme cascade, and at the end of the cascade, a crosslinked fibrin biopolymer is formed to plug the cut.

At each stage in the clotting cascade there is amplification, since one molecule catalyzes the production of many other molecules. This amplification allows for the fast production of a blood clot in order to quickly stop the loss of blood. Blood clotting incorporates thirteen different clotting factors.

Behe's argument focuses the fact that if one clotting factor in the cascade were eliminated, then the entire process would not work. People suffering from hemophilia, for example, lack the ability to produce one of the

---

14. Miller, *Finding*.

Why Intelligent Design Is Not Valid Science

clotting factors in the cascade. As a result, hemophiliacs can bleed to death from a simple cut.

On the surface, Behe's argument looks solid. Removing one step in the blood clotting cascade results in a process that does not work. Therefore, according to Behe, blood clotting is an example of an irreducibly complex system, which could not have been formed by many gradual modifications.

Miller considers the blood clotting system in detail, and he proposes a realistic hypothesis for how it could have evolved. His arguments are both detailed and persuasive. Miller draws heavily on the research of a molecular biologist, Russell Doolittle, who noted that all the clotting factor molecules are chemically similar to one another.[15]

The clotting factors are protein cutting enzymes, called serine proteases, which are found only in vertebrates, i.e., animals with a backbone such as humans and reptiles, and in crustaceans, e.g., crabs and lobsters. The modern blood clotting cascade could have evolved from a very simple process in which sticky white cells were the first clot forming systems that evolved. If only sticky white cells were used, then the primitive clotting system would work, but it would be slow. If serine proteases could be introduced into the bloodstream, they could really enhance this basic system.

Gene duplication is one of the mechanisms that evolution uses to achieve its objective. When a gene is duplicated, the duplicated gene is freed up (miss-targeted) for use in systems other than the one to which it was originally directed. This process is similar to repurposing Miller's tie clip to form part of a mouse trap.

Doolittle hypothesized that a gene that produced a serine protease enzyme was duplicated. Then, the target for the duplicated serine protease enzyme was altered so that it would work in the blood stream. As a result, an initial blood-based serine protease enzyme would have evolved.

Additional gene duplication, used this time for the production of another new blood-based serine protease, could then give rise to a second clotting factor, resulting in a more sensitive clotting system. After a number of such gene duplications the complex, multistage cascade system that exists today would have evolved. Given the 4.5-billion-year age of the Earth, enough time would be available for evolution to produce the thirteen clotting factors that exist today.

---

15. Doolittle, *Evolution*.

God the Geometer

A particularly interesting aspect of Doolittle's hypothesis is that it can be tested, whereas irreducible complexity cannot be tested. Vertebrates evolved from non-vertebrates, and Miller states:

> If the modern fibrinogen[16] gene really was recruited from a duplicated ancestral gene, one that had nothing to do with blood clotting, then we ought to be able to find a fibrinogen-like gene in an animal that does not possess the vertebrate clotting pathway.[17]

In fact, in 1990 Doolittle was co-author of a paper in which just such a molecule in the sea cucumber was identified.[18] Thus, it is plausible that the evolutionary ancestors of vertebrates had such a gene and it could be mistargeted to work in their bloodstream.

In his conclusion on blood clotting, Miller states:

> Now, it would not be fair, just because we have presented a realistic evolutionary scheme supported by gene sequences from modern organisms, to suggest that we know *exactly* how the clotting system has evolved. That would be making far too much of our limited ability to reconstruct the details of the past. Nonetheless, there is little doubt that we do know enough to develop a plausible—and scientifically valid—scenario for how it might have evolved. And that scenario makes specific predictions that can be tested and verified against evidence.[19]

Miller's arguments are lucid, sound, scientifically correct, and reasonable. He does an excellent job of refuting the argument of irreducible complexity and its use against evolution.

Coyne has given an interesting argument against ID. In an interview with Steve Mirsky he points out that humans have many non-functional pseudogenes that were functional in our ancestors. For example, humans cannot synthesize vitamin C[20] from simpler chemicals. However, humans do have a gene for synthesizing vitamin C, but as Coyne states:

---

16. Fibrinogen is a protein.
17. Miller, *Finding*, 158.
18. Xu, "Proceedings," 2097–101.
19. Miller, *Finding*, 158.
20. Vitamins are compounds containing carbon and other atoms required by the body for metabolism, protection, health, and growth. They cannot be synthesized by the body and must be obtained by outside sources, e.g. diet, Sun.

Why Intelligent Design Is Not Valid Science

> The most famous in our species is the gene for making vitamin C. And we have the complete pathway, but the last step, the genome involved in the last step of the process, is broken; it's dead because there is a part of the DNA sequence which has actually been removed or has been snipped out. And yet the gene is active in a lot of our relatives who use it to make vitamin C. Presumably humans don't need to do that because we have plenty of vitamin C in our diet and so the pathway was superfluous and it just sort of became inactivated by random mutation.[21]

The question for ID proponents is why would an intelligent designer create a vitamin C gene and then proceed to deactivate it? Such a process does not appear to be the result of intelligence at all. The same question can be raised for other pseudogenes.

Irreducible complexity is a God in the gaps approach to science, where God is invoked when science cannot explain some phenomena. What the ID proponents propose is a universe that is semi-autonomous in its design. Evolution goes along until a problem that it cannot address arises. At this point God directly intervenes in the evolutionary process and solves the problem. However, there is no scientific way that any of the proposed gap solutions can be studied, if in fact God solved the problem. That is why ID is referred to as pseudoscience. As science advances more and more of the gap arguments from ID proponents are being refuted.

Wikipedia points out:

> The ID movement has not published a properly peer-reviewed article supporting ID in a scientific journal, and has failed to publish supporting peer-reviewed research or data. The Discovery Institute [a proponent of ID] says that a number of ID articles have been published in peer-reviewed journals, but critics, largely members of the scientific community, reject this claim and state ID proponents have set up their own journals with peer review that lack impartiality and rigor, consisting entirely of ID supporters.[22]

Michael Behe is a faculty member in the Department of Biological Sciences at Lehigh University. On its website the Department has a statement on ID that concludes: "It is our collective position that ID has no basis in science, has not been tested experimentally, and should not be regarded

---

21. Mirsky, "Phrasing," para 10.
22. "Intelligent Design," Scientific criticism, para. 5.

as scientific."[23] The Department does support Behe's right to express his view on ID, but they unanimously do not support his view.

ID proponents believe that God intervenes to change the course of evolution. I believe that God does intervene in our universe, but in a different way. To avoid any confusion, I want to repeat statements I made in chapter 1 about God's intervention. I believe that physical miracles, due to God, occasionally happen, but they are very, very rare and by far the exception rather than the norm. I also believe that God regularly interacts with humans on a spiritual level. Miracles, for example, might involve a person being cured of a disease but they do not involve changing the course of evolution on the Earth.

ID proponents could ask why the interaction that occurs in miracles differs from the intervention in evolution proposed by them. The important distinction between miracles and ID is that there is actual physical evidence that a miracle has occurred and this evidence can be examined scientifically. For ID no such evidence exists, so no scientific judgement of it can be made. Further, it is not logical that would God reveal himself through miracles, but stay hidden in ID. In chapters 10 and 11 a number of miracles and the physical evidence for them are presented.

Since this chapter discusses a topic at odds with God's actual design, no insight into God's *design imperative* can be learned from ID. Current scientific knowledge indicates that God did not design a semi-automatous universe in which periodic intervention is required to change the course of evolution.

23. "Department," para. 2.

8

Free Will and Quantum Indeterminacy

KENNETH MILLER IN *FINDING Darwin's God*[1] has published one of the most interesting, penetrating, and important discussions of free will that I have read. I discuss Miller's insights in detail below. Miller's discussion centers around quantum physics, which I want to consider before presenting his discussion. "Quantum" can be defined as the smallest discrete unit of a phenomenon. For example, an electron is a quantum of electricity.

As Simon Singh states in the *Big Bang*: "Quantum physics is the most successful and utterly bizarre theories in the whole of physics."[2] Quantum physics is perhaps the most difficult field of science to explain to non-scientists, and in fact, even to scientists. Indeed, Nobel Laureate Richard Feynman has stated: "I think I can safely say that nobody understands quantum [physics] mechanics."[3] So, if readers have trouble with this chapter they should not fret. They are in very good company.

Quantum physics takes us into realms in which our everyday intuition simply doesn't hold. Quantum physics arose in the early 1900s as an attempt to explain the nature of light and the spectral radiation coming from atoms and molecules. This field of physics deals with small particles, molecules, atoms, and subatomic species. As atom smashers became more

---

1. Miller, *Finding*.
2. Singh, *Big*, 491.
3. Feynman, *Character*, 129.

and more powerful, more and more subatomic species were seen experimentally, leading to what physicists have termed the subatomic zoo. Today physicists talk about particles such as electrons, protons, neutrons, quarks, neutrinos, and muons, to name just a few.

To explain the behavior of these particles in high energy collision experiments and in astronomical measurements, physicists need to consider such things as virtual particles and antimatter. The virtual particles don't actually exist, but if they are not included in the theory then the theoretical predictions are wrong. If an antiparticle, which does exist, collides with its particle counterpart then both are destroyed and energy in the form of primarily photons is released. An example would involve an electron colliding with a positron.[4] The current theory of atomic and subatomic particles reads like the statement from *Alice in Wonderland*, "[it gets] curiouser and curiouser."[5]

Robert Oerter[6] gives an interesting hypothetical example to help sharpen the difference between what happens at the quantum level and at the macroscopic level that we deal with every day. His example, which is an analogy, illustrates both the quantum (discrete) nature and the probabilistic nature of matter. The example: a couple decides to paint their house. The husband prefers red for the color, and his wife blue. If the painter mixes the two colors, then in the macroscopic world the house would be painted purple.

In the microscopic world, even though the mixed paint were used, the house would only be red or blue, but never purple, since only the two premixed discrete colors are allowed. Further, there would be a probability of the house being either color. When the couple came home each day from work, they would find that the house was either red or blue, but never purple. The quantum world is indeed a strange place, with strange rules governing its behavior.

One actual experiment can be used to illustrate the strange behavior present in the microscopic quantum world. Figure 8.1 shows a setup for the famous double slit experiment. In Figure 8.1a a monochromatic light wave, e.g. generated by a laser, is shown passing through the two slits and

---

4. A PET (*Positron Emission Tomography*) scan employs positrons resulting from radioactive decay (nuclear fission). A PET scan is an effective way to help identify a variety of conditions, including cancer, heart disease and brain disorders.

5 Carroll, *Alice in Wonderland*, 9.

6. Oerter, *Theory*, 222–28.

impinging on an optical screen detector behind the slits. The optical screen detector could be a photographic film.

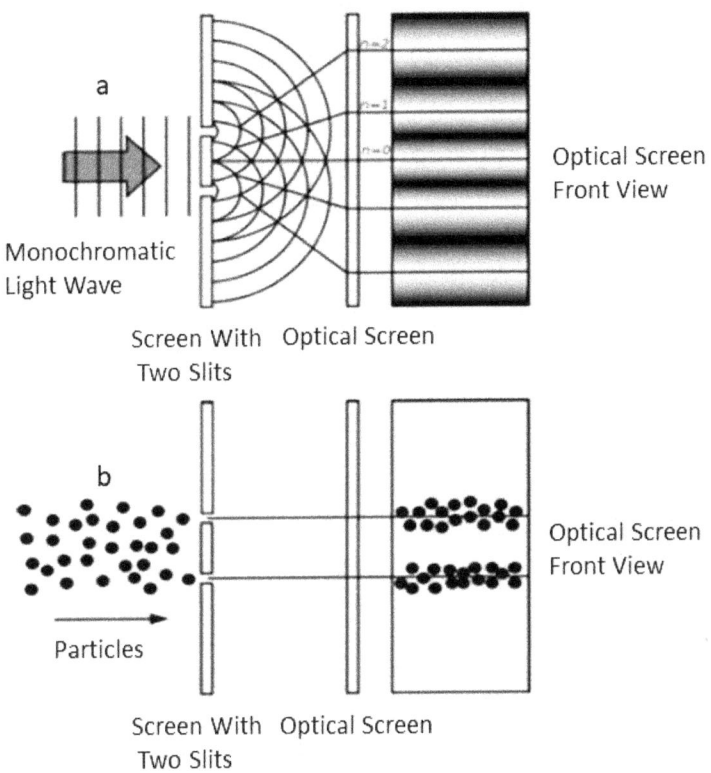

Figure 8.1. Double slit experimental setup.[7]

In Figure 8.1 a and b, the front view of what the optical screen measures is shown at the right. For the light wave the measured pattern is a series of bright and dark regions. This pattern involves interference and reinforcement from the light acting as a wave. If one throws a stone into the water the ripples that are seen in the water involve interference and reinforcement from pressure wave changes caused by the stone.

Figure 8.1b shows the pattern that would result if small particles were fired at the slits. If only a small number of particles are fired, then

7. "Double."

the detector in Figure 8.1b would show individual circles. After measuring many particles in this case, one would only see two dark lines which would be the same width as the slits. The circles show where each particle hit the detector.

What is interesting about this double slit experiment, is what happens if one tries to measure the light passing through the slits using two photometers. Before the measurement, the pattern is that shown in Figure 8.1a. Before the photometers are added light acts as a wave. As soon as photometers are added the pattern changes to that shown in Figure 8.1b. Adding the measurement devices causes the light to change from acting like a wave to acting like a particle!

In fact, light has a dual nature; it can act both as a particle as well as a wave. In our macroscopic world we do not experience a measurement changing the characteristics of what we see or experience. However, as the double slit experiment demonstrates, measurement can drastically change behavior in the quantum, microscopic world. No wonder Feynman said that "nobody understands quantum mechanics."

In his excellent book *Believing Is Seeing* Michael Guillen has an insightful and inspirational discussion on the equivalence of God and Light.[8] Guillen quotes the first letter of John which states: "God is light; in him there is no darkness at all" (1 John 5). Further, in John's Gospel Jesus says: "I am the light of the world. The person who follows me will never live in darkness but will have the light that gives life" (John 8:12). Also, in the Nicene Creed Jesus is described as: "God from God, Light from Light, true God from true God, begotten, not made, one in Being with the Father." Thus, Jesus and God are referred to as being Light."[9]

Light has the amazing property that its speed is the same when seen by any observer, no matter how fast the observer is moving relative to the light source. In *Believing Is Seeing* Michael Guillen discusses other remarkable properties of light and he compares what science says about light to what Christianity says about Light. The five properties that Guillen describes are: " Light is the embodiment of a contradiction; Light does not obey the rules of ordinary matter; Light can transform into matter, and vice versa; Light has a sacred status in the universe; and Light exists in a timeless world."[10]

---

8. Guillen, *Believing*, 45–53.
9. "Catholic."
10. Guillen, *Believing*, 50–53.

Free Will and Quantum Indeterminacy

The two slit experiment discussed above demonstrates the contradiction property in that light is both a particle and a wave. Guillen compares the contradiction property of light to Jesus being both mortal and immortal. Guillen compares the fact that light can be converted to matter to Christ's incarnation in which Light became matter through the Incarnation. Guillen also points out that at the speed of light time stops and light, "therefore, is not constrained by time." He further states: "God created time; so, he exists outside of it. God, therefore, is not constrained by time."[11] Thus, light possesses properties that are just as deep and confounding as those embodied in Christianity.

In spite of seemingly bizarre behavior at the atomic and subatomic level, there are rules and symmetries that govern how particles behave there. So, even in the very strange world of atomic and subatomic physics it is possible for physicists to develop hypotheses and test them via measurements, just as they have done in other fields. As of the present, no prediction made by quantum theory has proved to be wrong.

Today, researchers are studying quantum computation in order to try to harness the phenomena of quantum physics for solving problems more effectively than they can be solved using digital computers. Quantum computers offer a potential speed advantage over digital computers. It seems that in addition to the other knowledge humans have developed, we were meant to find out about this strange quantum world as well.

One particularly interesting aspect of quantum physics involves quantum indeterminacy. The Heisenberg Uncertainty Principle[12] (quantum indeterminacy), formulated in 1927 by Werner Heisenberg, states that at the level of elementary particles,[13] e.g. electrons, protons, atoms, and so on, we cannot know precisely both the particle's location and its momentum (particle's mass times its velocity). All we can know is the probability of its location and the probability of its momentum. After making his discovery Heisenberg wrote: "Can nature possibly be absurd as it seemed to us in these atomic experiments?"[14]

---

11. Guillen, *Believing*, 53.

12. Heisenberg, "Zeitschrift," 172–98.

13. E.g. electrons, protons, atoms, and so on. Heisenberg's principle applies to any sized object. For the large objects that we see around us the uncertainty is vanishingly small and it can safely be ignored. The uncertainty is only important for very small particles such as small molecules, atoms, and subatomic particles.

14. Herbert, *Quantum*, 55.

God the Geometer

The quantum world with its Heisenberg uncertainty exactly contradicts our everyday knowledge of the physical world. We see a table at an exact place in a room, and we know that it is stationary. Alternatively, we see a car moving, and we know where it is; if we had a radar gun we could measure how fast it is moving without changing its speed.

While we have a very clear picture of the macroscopic physical world around us, such a clear picture is *fundamentally* and *theoretically impossible* at the microscopic level of the elementary particles from which our universe is made. All that is possible is a probabilistic determination of location and momentum. For example, we might know that it is eighty percent probable that an electron is at a certain location. The electron might be at the location and it might not, just like the house might be red or blue on a given day. By contrast, we are one hundred percent certain where the table is in the room.

Particle uncertainty greatly troubled Albert Einstein, who was one of the founders of quantum mechanics. Einstein did not like the probabilistic nature of quantum mechanics, and he is quoted as having said: "God does not play dice"; to which Neils Bohr, another founder of quantum mechanics, replied: "Who is Einstein to tell God what to do?"[15]

Quantum indeterminacy powerfully demonstrates the unbelievable length to which our Creator went in designing a universe that allows for free will. Indeed, God does play dice at the microscopic level, and Miller does a brilliant job of explaining why this probabilistic nature must be so if true freedom is to exist in the world.

In addressing the problem faced by the Creator, Miller states:

> In constructing this physical world, the Creator faced a practical problem... How should the matter of this physical world behave, what rules should it follow? If the Creator made the behavior of this material world logical and sensible, He would ultimately allow His intelligent creatures to investigate the universe and discover the properties of the matter He has created. If the behavior of that matter, at all levels, were to be governed by laws making the outcomes of all natural processes inherently predictable, then the entire structure of the universe would be a self-contained and self-sufficient clockwork.... His creatures could not have the freedom He desired for them. How could they, if they were only machines,

---

15. Miller, *Finding*, 212.

Free Will and Quantum Indeterminacy

made up of bits and pieces of matter following precise laws? Worse still, they might eventually figure that out.[16]

Basically, what Miller is saying is that if we had *quantum determinacy*, every event in the universe would be completely predictable from one initial state. There would be absolutely no opportunity to change any outcome whatsoever. In such a universe there would be no possibility of freedom existing. Everything in such a universe would follow a set, predetermined path.

Miller goes on to explain the brilliant solution that the Creator used in his design in order to solve the problems just mentioned:

> His solution was to fashion a material universe in which the conditions of precise determinism do not apply. On the larger scale, He made the averaged behavior of matter sensible and predictable, making it possible to construct organisms and environments that work according to natural laws, which His creatures were sure to discover. Then He ensured that the behavior of the material fine structure of the universe was inherently unpredictable due to the multiple effects of quantum indeterminacy. This would allow His creatures to develop a science that applies to large scale interactions, but one that is forever forbidden from grasping the detailed behavior of the units from which the material world is fashioned. That, of course, is exactly the world in which we live.[17]

A logical question that one might ask at this point is: can events at a microscopic, quantum scale affect life on a macroscopic scale? Miller addresses this as well:

> The DNA molecule is structured in precisely a way that makes the behavior of individual atoms, even individual electrons, significant. When a mutation, a mistake in copying DNA, occurs, there are no intermediate chemical forms. One of four DNA bases is changed completely into another base, and that change has a direct (and possibly permanent) effect on the code script gene. As a result, events with quantum unpredictability, including cosmic ray movements, radioactive disintegration [nuclear fission], and even molecular copying errors, exert direct influences on the sequences of bases in DNA.[18]

---

16. Miller, *Finding*, 250–51.
17. Miller, *Finding*, 250–51.
18. Miller, *Finding*, 207.

Indeed, chemical reactions take place on a molecular level and they can be affected by quantum scale effects. I suspect that our thought processes are also affected by quantum scale effects, and these effects may explain how new ideas can pop into our head seemingly from nowhere. Miller demonstrates that quantum indeterminacy not only allows for the existence of free will, but it can significantly affect the world as we experience it. The world is not predestined to travel down one particular path; rather, God and humans can influence what happens in the future.

There is a saying that many believers use, particularly when they or a friend, experience difficulties in life. The saying is: "Everything happens for a reason." Alternatively, some believers will say "it's God's will" when difficulties arise.

In 2002 Rick Warren wrote *The Purpose Driven Life*.[19] The book sold millions of copies and was a huge best seller. There are many inspirational quotes in Warren's book and they contributed to its success. Warren's book no doubt had a very positive effect on its many readers. There is one quote from Warren that I would take issue with, and it has the flavor of everything happening for a reason. He said: "There's a Grand Designer behind everything. Your life is not a result of random chance, fate, or luck. There is a master plan."[20]

Warren uses the term random chance, and as discussed in chapter 5 there is a difference between random and chance events. Random events cannot be predicted while chance events have a probability of occurring. I would change the second sentence in Warren's quote to read: your life can be a result of chance, fate, or luck. At the quantum level probability reigns and as a result there is a chance that we can experience real problems in our life. These problems are not "God's will", but rather they arise because of the way freedom, through quantum indeterminacy, was built into the fabric of our universe.

In looking at life one can take two perspectives about how God interacts with his world. In the first, God controls everything, and it is from this perspective that natural evils, e.g., disease, earthquakes, etc., discussed in chapter 9, present a problem. Why would God allow natural evil to be present in our world? In the second perspective, God does not constantly intervene and he allows nature to take its course. However, God freely provides his grace to support humans in dealing with life's difficulties. On

---

19. Warren, *Purpose*.
20. Kowalski, "Eternal."

Free Will and Quantum Indeterminacy

rare occasions he also intervenes physically through miracles, which are discussed in chapters 10 and 11.

I believe that the church needs to intensify its past efforts examining how God interacts with nature. He has given humans the intelligence and freedom to help shape the direction that nature takes, and to overcome disease, and other problems faced by mankind. I believe it will take time for the church to more fully integrate what we have learned from modern science, e.g., quantum indeterminacy, into its theology about how God interacts with nature. However, changes in the church's teachings happen slowly and it is good that they take time and are not done in haste.

So, the second perspective forces one to look anew at traditional beliefs rather than leading to some of the easy answers that the first perspective does. One does not find it comforting to realize that a chance happening such as an earthquake, a storm, or disease can affect one's life or the lives of loved ones. Most of us long to have a God who protects us from such evils. In 2 Corinthians St. Paul describes the thorn in the flesh that he experienced:

> So that I would not become too proud of the wonderful things that were shown to me, a painful physical problem was given to me. This problem was a messenger from Satan, sent to beat me and keep me from being too proud. I begged the Lord three times to take this problem away from me. But he said to me, "My grace is enough for you. When you are weak, my power is made perfect in you." So, I am very happy to brag about my weaknesses. Then Christ's power can live in me" (2 Cor 12:7–9).

God's grace can similarly help those facing life's difficulties due to chance events.

There was one question that I had after reading Miller's insightful book. It concerned his view on the existence of the human soul. So, I emailed Professor Miller, and he replied by cutting and pasting his answer into my original email. Here is his reply with my questions shown in italics and his answers in normal text.[21]

> *I am reading your book Finding Darwin's God and I am enjoying it very much. I don't know if you answer questions on the book but I thought I would try. I am a Catholic and I believe that you are right on target in terms of your description of evolution. However, I noted that on page 214 you write that life does not require a spirit. Correct.*

---

21. Miller, "Personal."

But the context of that is that life, being a material phenomenon, is self-sufficient. "Remember man, thou art dust and to dust thou shalt return." So, we need not look for spiritual explanations of how cells divide or how genes work. Material ones will do just fine.

I am wondering what your concept is of the soul, and the next life? Do you think that these exist? I think that the soul is the spiritual reflection, a spiritual mirror, of the thoughts and personality and individuality that are built into each of us. So, yes, I think that the soul is real, and yes, I have faith in the promise of an afterlife.

This chapter on quantum indeterminacy demonstrates the enormous importance that the Creator attached to human freedom and the extraordinary lengths that he was willing to go to achieve it as a key part of his *design imperative*. Miller's discussion of the effect that the microscopic world can have on our macroscopic world is truly insightful. We live in a world where everything does not happen for a reason, and chance events can affect our lives.

9

Freedom and Natural Evil

JOSEPH KELLY DISCUSSES EVIL in the world in his book, *The Problem of Evil in the Western Tradition. From the Book of Job to Modern Genetics.*[1] Kelly splits evil into that caused by humans, namely moral evil, and that which occurs in nature, namely natural evil. He defines moral evil as: "the deliberate imposition of suffering by a human being upon another sentient being."[2] A sentient being could be another human or even an animal.

Natural evil involves harm done by such things as storms, earthquakes, floods, disease, and carnivorous animals. What is the reason that these things are in the world? Are these things really evil, and why do humans have to deal with them? If disease, famine, floods, and earthquakes are called acts of God, then what is God's purpose in allowing them to happen? These are questions that have puzzled human beings since they appeared on the Earth.

I became interested in why natural evil exists in the world when my wife of almost forty-two years, Jessie, passed away from a rare, and debilitating cancer, pseudomyxoma peritonei (PMP).[3] PMP causes very large mucinous tumors to grow in the peritoneal cavity, which lead to death through starvation. The tumors grow to a point where patients cannot

1. Kelly, *Problem*.
2. Kelly, *Problem*, 3.
3. O'Connell, "American," 551–64.

process food, and if they eat they throw up. They are literally crushed from inside out. Although a patient can be kept alive by getting a glucose solution intravenously, this feeding only prolongs the eventual outcome of the disease. I questioned why such a horrible disease as PMP existed in our world. To seek an answer, I began to do a lot of reading both on natural evil and on science.

One of the books that I read that helped with my grief was a huge best-seller written by Rabbi Harold Kushner, *When Bad Things Happen to Good People*.[4] I found this book so captivating that I read it in three days. Kushner had a son, Aaron, who was diagnosed when he was only three years old with a genetic disease called progeria. This disease results in rapid aging. The Kushners were told that Aaron would not grow to be more than three feet tall; he would look like a little old man and die in his early teens.

It is impossible to imagine the amount of pain and suffering that such a diagnosis causes for parents. After Aaron's passing, Rabbi Kushner wrote his book and dedicated it to Aaron. In the book he describes many of the encounters he has had with members of his congregation and others during his ministry. He describes the insights into life he has gained, particularly in light of his son's disease and premature death. Rabbi Kushner's insights are discussed below.

In the book of Genesis in the Old Testament there are two creation stories. The first story on the days of creation indirectly addresses the issue of natural evil in the world. Near the end of the first Genesis creation story there is a verse that talks about what the humans and animals will eat: "I have given all the green plants as food for every wild animal, every bird of the air, and every small crawling animal" (Gen 1:30). From this statement one gets the impression that animals were created to be herbivores, and they were not carnivorous.

Humans also are given fruit and seeds to eat. Yet, fossil records show that early animals were indeed carnivorous, as were humans. The fossil record is not an issue if one views the first creation story as mythological in nature and not as an historical or scientific description. However, the Genesis text seems to be an attempt to explain away the fact that some animals are indeed carnivorous, and they kill and eat other animals.

The second creation story is the well-known Adam and Eve story, and it is independent from the first creation story. The second story talks about the place in which Adam and Eve lived, the Garden of Eden. Although the

---

4. Kushner, *When Bad Things Happen*.

Freedom and Natural Evil

Garden of Eden was a paradise, man had to work the Garden and care for it. Adam is told not to eat of the fruit of the tree of the knowledge of good and evil. It is interesting that evil is associated with this tree even before humans disobey God, resulting in a number of natural evils coming into the world. It is also very interesting that God would not want humans to gain knowledge about good and evil.

Eve and then Adam eat the forbidden fruit, and as a result they are banished from Eden. The Bible the tells us what the result of eating the forbidden fruit will be:

> Then God said to the woman, "I will cause you to have much trouble when you are pregnant, and when you give birth to children, you will have great pain. You will greatly desire your husband, but he will rule over you." Then God said to the man, "You listened to what your wife said, and you ate fruit from the tree from which I commanded you not to eat. "So, I will put a curse on the ground, and you will have to work very hard for your food. In pain you will eat its food all the days of your life. The ground will produce thorns and weeds for you, and you will eat the plants of the field. You will sweat and work hard for your food. Later you will return to the ground, because you were taken from it. You are dust, and when you die, you will return to the dust" (Gen 3:16–19).

Thus, the text attributes weeds, thorns, pain in childbirth, and death to man's sin of disobedience, a moral evil. In fact, weeds, thorns, pain in childbirth, and death were certainly built into the Earth at its creation.

So, both creation stories try to explain away some aspects of what could be called natural evil as either not present at the time of creation (creation story 1), or as being caused by human disobedience (creation story 2). Since the creation stories are not historical, these details do not need to match what is known from science. However, one can ask if there is any message in these details. It seems that the writers of the creation stories want to convey the idea that God did not create the world as we know it. Our knowledge from science contradicts and disagrees with this message. What theology has termed natural evil, science suggests was built into the world from its beginning, prior to humans coming on the scene.

After Jessie's passing I attended an evening theology class at my parish. I wanted to gain insight into why diseases such as PMP exist in our world. The class was taught by Deacon Anthony Norcio, who was a Professor of Information Systems at the University of Maryland Baltimore County. Anthony had an impressive and broad academic background, with a B.A.

degree in economics, a B.S. degree in statistics, an M.L.S. degree in information science, and a Ph.D. in psychology. He also had an M.A. degree in systematic theology, and two graduate certificates in biblical studies and advanced biblical studies.

Two of the evening theology sessions were on natural and moral evil, and they were the ones that I was most interested in. A week or two before these sessions, on the day after Christmas, 2004, there was a powerful tsunami that struck Southeast Asia. Over one hundred and eighty thousand people died, with one hundred and thirty thousand people missing and presumed dead due to the resulting flooding. There was unbelievable destruction over the entire region, and the tsunami was felt even as far away as the coast of Africa. Several million people lost their homes and livelihoods.

Deacon Norcio suggested that this catastrophe, as well as several other things like disease and hurricanes, could be classified as natural evils. He then asked what the Bible or theology tells us about the cause of natural evils. His answer was that the issue of what causes natural evil is not discussed in the Bible or by theologians, other than the Garden of Eden story in Genesis. This answer was particularly disappointing to me. Here is a key issue that according to Deacon Norcio is simply not addressed by theologians, who focus primarily on causes of moral evil.

In my opinion one can learn as much about God's nature by studying natural evil as by studying moral evil. With moral evil humans are involved, and their involvement makes it more difficult to gain insight into God's nature. By contrast, only God is involved with what has been labeled natural evil. If one can gain insight into why natural evil exists in the world, one thereby gains direct insight into the nature of God, and his *design imperative* in creating the universe.

The last word in the *design imperative*, namely optimally, indicates that the final design should be the best possible. Here we have to have faith that God created the very best universe in which humans could live, express their freedom, and have the opportunity to grow and be successful. Such a universe would also allow God to occasionally intervene physically, provided that such intervention did not compromise human freedom.

Consider the 2004 tsunami. Tsunamis are caused by earthquakes that result from tectonic plate motion on the Earth's surface. To stop tsunamis, one would have to eliminate tectonic plate motion. However, as discussed in chapter 4 tectonic plate motion helps regulate the Earth's temperature. Tectonic plate motion also produces continents, high ground, and mountain ranges. Since the Earth has so much water on it, without tectonic plate motion the land would be flat and the Earth's surface would be underwater. Life on Earth as we know it would impossible. One might then say, let's have an Earth with less water on it, but that condition would also lead to problems for life as we know it. Designing a universe like the one we live in is an unbelievably complex task that involves a myriad of conflicting considerations and tradeoffs.

To be able to achieve everlasting life we need to be free to make decisions, and our decisions have to have real meaning. The greatest gift that God gives us is our free will, and it is up to us to use it effectively. Since God did not choose to constantly intervene physically, he used an *autonomous design* for our universe, in which humans would have real freedom to affect their future. As with all designs, tradeoffs arose from trying to meet the *objective* while satisfying the *solution constraints*. I believe that it is these tradeoffs that gave rise to the dualistic nature of the universe, in which we can easily see good and natural evil all around us.

Consider the Adam and Eve creation story and assume that the first humans did not eat the forbidden fruit. What would life have been like in the Garden of Eden? If we look at what happened as a result of eating the fruit we can reconstruct what life would have been like before the fall. Although Adam would have had to work the land, his work would have been relatively easy since there would have been no thorns or weeds. Eve would not have experienced pain in childbirth, and neither Adam nor Eve would die.

Is this the type of physical paradise in which we would want to live? What sense of accomplishment would Adam and Eve have felt if everything was taken care of for them? Would they really have been happy in such an environment? In the Garden of Eden there would be no pain or suffering, but would there be any real freedom? Would there be any real sense of accomplishment? I don't think so. We need to be truly free to feel that we have accomplished something.

I believe that this is the explanation of natural evil: that because creation was constrained to be both free and physical, good and evil are inherent in the Creator's design of the universe. It is how we deal with dualistic tradeoffs, which inevitably occur in our lives, that is important. Life is a test and how we do on the test in this life will determine what happens in the next life.

God the Geometer

Job was tested when he lost his family, possessions, and health: "I cry out to you, God, but you do not answer; I stand up, but you just look at me. You have turned on me without mercy; with your powerful hand you attacked me" (Job 30:20–21). St. Paul was tested with a thorn in the flesh:

> So that I would not become too proud of the wonderful things that were shown to me, a painful physical problem was given to me. This problem was a messenger from Satan, sent to beat me and keep me from being too proud. I begged the Lord three times to take this problem away from me. But he said to me, "My grace is enough for you. When you are weak, my power is made perfect in you." So, I am very happy to brag about my weaknesses. Then Christ's power can live in me (2 Cor 12:7–9).

Even Christ was tested to the point of asking on the cross why God had abandoned him: "At three o'clock Jesus cried in a loud voice, 'Eloi, Eloi, lama sabachthani.' This means, 'My God, my God, why have you rejected me?'" (Mark 30:34).

These passages point out just how real and deep the testing we experience is. If Job, St. Paul, and Jesus were tested so profoundly, why should we be immune to testing? Testing is a built-in part of our physical existence in which we have to deal with tradeoffs. The greatest gift humans have is our free will, which we can use to pass the tests of this life. It is in the next life that we will know our test scores.

One of the great quotes from Joseph Kelly's book is: "the only way to truly know something is to know its opposite."[5] In order really to appreciate happiness we have to experience sadness. To know the real meaning of love we have to see what hate can do. To appreciate fellowship with others we need to experience loneliness. When I lost Jessie, I knew what it meant to be lonely, and I appreciate much more now what she meant to me.

So, it seems to me that for life to be truly meaningful we have to experience opposites, and that implies that we have to have true freedom to make choices. We would not be truly happy if God completely controlled our behavior and made all the decisions for us. We certainly need to ask his help and guidance, but ultimately, we have to have the freedom to live our lives ourselves. We have to make use of our free will. Then, when we accomplish something or overcome some obstacle in life we can be truly proud of what we have done. I might add that God can take pride in his handiwork as well.

5. Kelly, *Problem*, 250–51.

Freedom and Natural Evil

Now consider the effect that quantum indeterminacy, discussed in chapter 8, can have in causing molecular copying errors. Evolutionary change takes place through genetic mutations; gene mutations allow for new species to emerge and for evolution to move forward without constant intervention by the Creator. Mutation is necessary for life to evolve freely, but mutations can lead to diseases like PMP, cancer, and progeria. Without genetic mutations there would be no mechanism that would allow for evolution to move forward in a completely free and independent manner.

The necessity of mutation and its results can be an extremely difficult tradeoff to accept by those who have seen its negative results. As Ruse states in *Can A Darwinian Be A Christian*:

> There are some mutations which have quite horrendous effects, causing the most devastating of physical and psychological illnesses. Young children compulsively mutilating themselves, for instance, wracked by pain, their mental deficiencies depriving them of any chance of happiness and a normal life. Is eternal bliss for any of us—that child, the Pope, Mother Theresa, you or me—worth the suffering of that child? Dare one say yes?[6]

Ruse's question is a very difficult, in fact almost impossible question to answer in the affirmative. When I recall all that Jessie went through with PMP I have great difficulty answering yes. I feel certain that Rabbi Kushner would say the same thing about the progeria that afflicted his son Aaron. It is very difficult for humans to comprehend all of the tradeoffs that were involved with the design of the universe as we know it. At some point we have to accept on faith the fact that the Designer created an optimal universe, in which we could live, be truly free, and have the opportunity to behave in a way to gain everlasting life.

In his book Rabbi Kushner states:

> I believe in God. But I do not believe the same things about Him that I did years ago, when I was growing up or when I was a theological student. I recognize His limitations. He is limited in what He can do by laws of nature and by the evolution of human nature and moral freedom. I no longer hold God responsible for illnesses, accidents, and natural disasters, because I realize that I gain little and I lose so much when I blame God for those things.[7]

---

6. Ruse, *Can*, 139.
7. Kushner, *When*, 134.

God the Geometer

I basically agree in principle with Kushner, who I feel has a great deal of insight into the meaning of life. However, I don't think that limited is the right word to use to describe God. God's limitations, in my opinion, stem from his self-imposed *solution constraint* not to interfere continuously in our universe. He allows mankind the freedom to affect the world in which we live.

God set the laws of nature in motion when the Big Bang occurred. He could have directly created our universe as we now know it. Had God done so we would not have been able to use our intelligence to make hypotheses and carry out measurements to understand his design. Rather, God set in motion natural processes, and he allows them to take their course. From time to time he definitely has intervened in nature and miracles, discussed in chapters 10 and 11, have occurred. But these physical instances are rare. The norm seems to be that the laws of nature hold just about all the time. I also believe that God through grace intervenes regularly in our world, by inspiring humans at the spiritual level.

I do not think that Rabbi Kushner feels that God is not infinitely powerful or that he is insensitive to our prayers. I think, rather, that he is stating the fact that by and large God chooses not to intervene in the universe that he created so that humans can be truly free to act on their own.

For myself, I would slightly rephrase Kushner's sentences and state: I believe in God. But I do not believe the same things about him that I did years ago, when I was growing up. I recognize God's hand in the design and evolution of the universe, including the resulting tradeoffs. He chooses to respect the laws of nature and the evolution of human nature and moral freedom. I no longer hold God responsible for illnesses, accidents, and natural disasters, because I realize that I gain little and I lose so much when I blame God for those things.

Throughout this chapter insights into God's *design imperative* for our universe have been pointed out. I believe that natural evil is not evil per se, but it results from the tradeoffs inherent in the design of our universe. Natural evil is simply nature.

10

Healing Miracles

IN BOTH THE OLD and New Testaments of the Bible miracles are discussed. This chapter focuses on healing miracles, and the next chapter other types of physical miracles. The word miracle comes from the Latin word miraculum, which means object of wonder. Merriam Webster defines a miracle as: "an extraordinary event manifesting divine intervention in human affairs."[1] In very rare instances, e.g. when a medical cure occurs, God gets involved with the physical universe in an obvious way by overriding physical laws. In other instances, which happen regularly, God intervenes with humans in a spiritual way with his grace, which is much less obvious.

Father Louis Monden wrote *Signs and Wonders* and it has an interesting chapter on the meaning of the miraculous. Father Monden states:

> On the assumption that God were to create a purely natural world order, sound theology can give no good reason why miracles should occur. For such an order is verified precisely in the constancy and regularity of the course of events. Would not any change wrought in it by God, whether intended as a remedy for some malfunctioning in the order—if such may be admitted in view of God's omnipotence!—or as a capricious display of power, be an occasion of disorder in the universe and a contradiction of God's wisdom?[2]

1. "Miracle."
2. Monden, *Signs*, chap. 2.

God the Geometer

The question raised by Father Monden assumes that chance does not play a part in world order. However, as discussed in chapter 5 chance does play an important part in evolution, and it leads to some non-constancy and disorder in the course of events. As discussed in chapter 8, quantum indeterminacy means that perfect world order here on Earth is not possible. As a result, God can perform miracles and they are not an occasion of disorder, or a contradiction of God's wisdom.

Miracles are outside the realm covered by science. In spite of the physical evidence for the occurrence of miracles, many scientists dismiss them out of hand and believe that they are not possible. Father Andrew Apostoli has an interesting comment on this point: "For those with faith, no explanation is necessary. For those without faith no explanation is possible."[3] The proper approach that scientists should take in studying miracles is to first look at the physical evidence for their occurrence. Then, if the miracle cannot be explained scientifically, they should simply say so, but not deny the physical evidence of a miracle.

I believe that miracles provide "data" for the existence of God. I put data in quotations because of the nature of miracles. When one generates scientific data, normally multiple experiments are run and the results compared to one another to verify or reject a particular theory. Miracles are rare, one off events, which are not repeated. Even though they are not repeated one can examine the facts involved in a miracle and ask whether they demonstrate that there is a very high probability that physical laws could have been overridden. If physical laws have been overridden then this fact provides "data" for God's existence even though the identical miracle is not repeated, like a science experiment would be.

In the New Testament many healing miracles are described.[4] Jesus cures the blind, lepers, paralytics, a woman with a bleeding problem, and Peter's mother-in-law. He also raises Lazarus from the dead, cures a man with dropsy, another man with a withered hand, a deaf mute, and a centurion's servant, among others. The gospels also include other accounts of Jesus' power over nature, e.g. walking on water, feeding the multitude, etc. Indeed, it is the miracles that Jesus performed that no doubt attracted the crowds to him. It is easy to dismiss these miracles by saying that they occurred such a long time ago and there is really no way to check the validity

---

3. Apostoli, *Fátima*, 134.
4. "Miracles of Jesus."

Healing Miracles

of what has been reported. It is through faith that Christians believe that these miracles occurred as described.

The situation is different with modern miracles. Such miracles have been reported in a number of places, including Lourdes in France, and Fátima in Portugal. The evidence for modern miracles has been reported and documented, and it can be accessed. In this chapter I want to focus on Lourdes because of the excellent documentation that has been done at this site.

In 1858 between February 11 and July 16, the Virgin Mary appeared 18 times to Bernadette Soubirous, who was canonized Saint Bernadette. Bernadette was a poor peasant girl who lived the town of Lourdes. During one of the apparitions Mary instructed Bernadette to dig a hole and subsequently spring water flowed out of it. From the very beginning of the spring, miraculous curative powers have been attributed to this water and to the Lourdes site.

In his book, *Healing Fire of Christ*[5], Father Paul Glynn documents over a dozen healing miracles that have occurred at Lourdes, or have been associated with Lourdes. In this chapter I will focus on one particular healing miracle, discussed by Glynn, which involved the cure of John Traynor. Traynor's miracle is an amazing story, but the other miracles that Glynn describes are equally amazing, e.g. those of Gabriel Gargam, and Jeanne Fretel.

Wikipedia describes the history of the investigations of Lourdes' miracles.[6] The earliest investigations of miracles at Lourdes were carried out by an Episcopal Commission of Inquiry reporting to the local bishop. Initially the Episcopal Commission had only clergy, and no medical members. In 1859, Professor Henri Vergez, a faculty member in the School of Medicine at Montpellier, was appointed medical consultant to the Episcopal Commission. Professor Vergez's views about a miracle often were different than those of the clergy. Professor Vergez felt that of the early cases considered only eight should be labeled miracles.

In 1883 the Medical Bureau of the Sanctuary was established. The objective of the Medical Bureau was: "so that no one, who thought he had been 'cured', would leave Lourdes without having submitted the story of his cure to a rigorous and collegiate medical assessment."[7] In 1905 the Holy See

---

5. Glynn, *Healing*.
6. "Lourdes Medical-1," para. 2.
7. "Lourdes," History.

(Pope Pius X) confirmed to the Bishop of Tarbes in his capacity as Guardian of the Grotto, the right to use the procedures of the Medical Bureau to investigate any declared cures. This right is still valid today.

In 1954 an international committee (International Medical Committee of Lourdes (CMIL) was established in order to expand the scope of Lourdes medical investigations. If the Medical Bureau decides that further investigation of a potential cure is called for, the case is referred to the CMIL. The CMIL, which meets annually, is a committee of about twenty medical experts in various specialties and its members have different religious beliefs.

For a cure to be recognized as medically inexplicable, the following facts need to be established:

> The original diagnosis must be verified and confirmed beyond doubt; the diagnosis must be regarded as "incurable" with current means (although ongoing treatments do not disqualify the cure); the cure must happen in association with a visit to Lourdes, typically while in Lourdes or in the vicinity of the shrine itself (although drinking or bathing in the water are not required); the cure must be immediate (rapid resolution of symptoms and signs of the illness); the cure must be complete (with no residual impairment or deficit); and the cure must be permanent (with no recurrence). CMIL is not entitled to pronounce a cure 'miraculous'; this must be done by the Church. The bureau may only pronounce that a cure is 'medically inexplicable'. A full investigation takes a minimum of five years (in order to ensure that the cure is permanent), and may take as long as ten or twelve years.[8]

At present, only seventy cures from Lourdes have been officially recognized by the Catholic Church as miraculous. No doubt numerous additional cures have occurred between 1858 and the present time. Even so, the number is very, very small compared to the number of people who have visited Lourdes seeking a cure.

The most recent Lourdes miracle was declared in February 2018, about ten years after its occurrence.[9] Sister Bernadette Moriau had suffered for over 40 years with spinal complications. She was eventually diagnosed with cauda equina syndrome, a disorder of the nerves and lower spine. Sister Moriau had been wheelchair-bound and fully disabled since 1980. She

---

8. "Lourdes Medical-2." Investigation of Apparent Cures.
9. Whitaker, "France's."

Healing Miracles

also had been taking morphine to control the pain. Sister Moriau took a pilgrimage to Lourdes in February, 2008. She was cured after returning to her community and has written a book, *My Life Is a Miracle*, describing her miraculous cure.[10]

Given the thorough, scientific, rigorous examination procedure followed at Lourdes, the position of skeptical scientists that miracles are impossible can be rejected. Only two logical explanations for the healing miracles at Lourdes can be given. The first is that they are caused by God. The second is that they are caused by some unknown physical process that we do not understand at present. Given the number and diversity of the reported cures I believe that they are caused by God.

Next the cure of John Traynor is discussed. The Reverend Patrick O'Conner encountered John Traynor at a train station in France in 1937. He rode with John for ten hours on the train from Lourdes to Paris. During that ride he talked with John about what had taken place fourteen years before in Lourdes. Subsequently he verified what John had told him.

Reverend O'Conner's detailed report (I Met A Miracle) was originally published by St. Columban's Foreign Mission Society in 1944. It is used with permission of the Mission Society of St. Columban and the Catholic Truth Society which holds the copyright to Reverend O'Connor's report.[11] Here what happened to John Traynor, as described by Reverend O'Conner, is presented. Reverend O'Conner's first person written account has been converted to the third person and significantly shortened. The interested reader can consult Reverend O'Conner's report for full details. Many of these details are not only enlightening but they are truly inspirational as well.

John Traynor was born and reared in Liverpool. His Irish mother died when he was still quite young, but her faith, her devotion to Mass and Holy Communion, and her trust in the Blessed Mother stayed with him as a memory and a fruitful example. The first world war broke out in 1914, and Jack Traynor was mobilized with the Royal Naval Reserve, to which he belonged. During a battle in Belgium, he was carrying one of his officers to safety, when he was hit on the head by shrapnel. He did not regain consciousness until five weeks later, when he woke up after an operation in a marine hospital in England. He recovered rapidly and went back into service.

10. Moriau, *My Life*.
11. O'Connor, "I Met."

God the Geometer

On April 25th, 1915, he took part in the landing at Gallipoli, Turkey. He was in charge of the first boat to leave the ship and was one of the few to reach the shore that day. Traynor took part in the battle, without injury, until May 8th, when he was hit by machine gun fire during a bayonet charge. He was wounded in the head and chest, and a bullet tore through the inner side of his upper right arm and lodged under the collar bone. The nerves in John's right arm were severed, and over the years he underwent four unsuccessful operations aimed at restoring the use of his arm.

In 1915 John suffered his first epileptic attack, which resulted from his earlier shrapnel wound. In April, 1920, Traynor was operated on in an attempt to alleviate his epilepsy, but the surgery did not help. The operation left Traynor with an open hole about an inch wide in his skull, and a silver plate was inserted to shield his brain.

John was discharged from military service, first on 80 percent pension, then raised to 100 percent and listed as being permanently and completely disabled. John suffered epileptic fits that were as frequent as three a day. Both legs were partly paralyzed, and nearly every organ in Traynor's body was impaired.

In the month of July, 1923, John was at home, helpless as usual, when a neighbor came by and spoke of an announcement that had been made in their parish. A Liverpool diocesan pilgrimage to Lourdes was being organized. John scraped up the thirteen pound fee for the pilgrimage and registered to go. One of the priests in charge of the pilgrimage came to John twice and strongly tried to convince him not to go. Everyone with the exception of his wife and one or two relatives told him he was crazy to go.

The newspapers in Liverpool heard about John's determination to go to Lourdes and he became somewhat of a celebrity. Figure 10.1 shows a photo from the Liverpool ECHO newspaper of John at the train station before leaving on the pilgrimage.

Healing Miracles

Figure 10.1. Jack Traynor the invalid leaving for Lourdes,
July 21, 1923, Lime Street Station, Liverpool.

John reached Lourdes on July 22nd, and he was transferred with the rest of the sick to the Asile Hospital at the Grotto. He was in a terrible condition, with wounds and sores that had not been freshly bandaged since he left Liverpool.

John spent six days in Lourdes, and during that time, he was desperately ill. John had several hemorrhages as well as epileptic fits. In spite of his condition, however, he succeeded in being bathed nine times in the water from the Grotto spring and he was taken to the different devotions in which the sick could join.

On the morning of the second day John had a bad epileptic fit as he was being wheeled to the baths. Blood flowed from his mouth and the doctors were very much alarmed. They wanted to take him back to the Asile Hospital at once. John protested and he put the brake on his wheel chair using his good hand, the left one. The volunteer stretcher bearers (brancardiers) took him into the baths and bathed him in the usual way. He never had an epileptic fit after that.

On July 24th Drs. Azurdia, Finn and Marley, who had come with the pilgrimage, examined Traynor at Lourdes. Their signed statement is on record. It testifies that they found him to be suffering from:

1. Epilepsy ["we ourselves saw several attacks during his journey to Lourdes"]
2. Paralysis of the radial, median, and ulnar nerves of the right arm
3. Atrophy of the shoulder and pectoral muscles
4. A trephine opening in the right parietal region of the skull; in this opening, about 2.5 cm, there is a metal plate for protection
5. Absence of voluntary movement in the legs and loss of feeling
6. Lack of bodily control

On July 26, John was wheeled down to the baths again. When he was in the baths, his paralyzed legs became violently agitated. The brancardiers became alarmed once more, thinking that he was having another seizure. The brancardiers clothed John hurriedly, put him back on the stretcher and rushed him down to the square in front of the Rosary Church to await a procession of the Blessed Sacrament.

The Blessed Sacrament had just passed when John realized that a great change had taken place in him. His right arm, which had been dead since 1915, was violently agitated. He burst the bandages on his right arm and blessed himself for the first time in years. John attempted to rise from his stretcher, but the brancardiers were watching him and restrained him.

Immediately after the final benediction they rushed him back to the Asile Hospital. John told them that he could walk, and proved it by taking seven steps. They put me back in bed and sedated him. Drs. Azurdia, Finn and Marley certify that they examined Traynor on his return to the Asile Hospital after the procession of the Blessed Sacrament. The doctors found that he had recovered the voluntary use of his legs, and his reflexes. There is intense venous congestion of both feet, which is very painful. The patient can walk with difficulty. Two brancardiers were stationed outside John's room to watch him.

John slept a bit and later in the evening, he jumped out of bed, and pushed the two brancardiers aside. He then ran down to the Grotto. Dr Marley was outside the door. When he saw the man over whom he had been watching during the pilgrimage, and whose death he had expected, push two brancardiers aside and run out of the ward, he fell back in amazement.

Out in the open now, John ran towards the Grotto, which is about two or three hundred yards from the Asile Hospital. This stretch of ground was graveled then, not paved, and John was barefoot. He ran the whole

Healing Miracles

way to the Grotto without getting the least mark or cut on his bare feet. The brancardiers were running after him but they could not catch up with him. When they reached the Grotto, there he was on his knees, still in his night clothes, praying to Our Lady and thanking her. All he knew was that he should thank her and the Grotto was the place to do it. The brancardiers stood back, afraid to touch him.

Early in the morning of July 27th the three doctors examined Traynor before the pilgrimage left Lourdes for home. Their statement says that:

1. He can walk perfectly
2. He has recovered the use and function of his right arm
3. He has recovered sensation in his legs
4. The opening in his skull has diminished considerably
5. There have been no more epileptic crises

Meanwhile the news of the miracle had been telegraphed to the Liverpool papers. Figure 10.2 below is a photo in the Liverpool ECHO of John arriving home and pushing his wheelchair!

Figure 10.2. Jack Traynor arriving home from Lourdes.

God the Geometer

After his cure John worked in the coal and haulage business. He had four trucks and about a dozen men working for him. He was able to lift sacks of coal weighing around two hundred pounds with the best of the men and he could do any other work that an able-bodied man could do. John went to Lourdes every year and worked as a brancardier there.

On July 7th, 1926, Traynor was examined again at Lourdes by Dr. Vallet, president of the Medical Bureau, together with five other doctors, Drs. Azurdia, Finn and Marley of Liverpool, who had examined him before and after his cure in 1923, Dr. Harrington of Preston, and Dr. Moorkens of Antwerp. They found no trace of epilepsy or paralysis. His right arm was completely free from atrophy. The pectoral and shoulder muscles were fully restored. His wrist worked normally and he could use his right hand. The official report, issued by the Medical Bureau at Lourdes on October 2nd, 1926, declared that this extraordinary cure is absolutely beyond and above the powers of nature.

The most striking part of this multiple miracle is probably the instantaneous cure of the right arm. The nerves had been severed for eight years. Four surgical operations had revealed that they were truly severed and had failed to reunite them. More than mere suture would be necessary before the arm could feel and move again; the shrunken nerves would need to go through a long process of regeneration. A feat that expert surgery had failed four times to do and a process that requires months of gradual restoration were achieved instantaneously as the Blessed Sacrament was raised over John Traynor.

Another group of experts testified, though unconsciously to the miracle. These were the doctors and officials of the War Pensions Ministry. These gentlemen, after years of examination, treatment, and inspection, certified that John Traynor was incurable. They showed the strength of their conviction by awarding him full disability pension for life. They never revoked that decision.

In corroborating Traynor's story Father O'Conner read the Liverpool newspaper reports, obtained the photos from the Liverpool ECHO, shown in Figures 10.1 and 10.2, and read the Medical Bureau reports signed by six doctors. In addition, the British War Ministry certified John Traynor as incurable. The evidence for this physical miracle is overwhelming.

To say that Traynor's cure did not occur is simply not believable. How did it occur? I believe that there are only two logical ways to look at his

Healing Miracles

cure: either it was a true healing miracle, or it was caused by as yet some unknown force.

Scientists who are agnostics or atheists, and who take the time to examine the facts discussed above, would propose the unknown force as the answer. These same scientists would believe in the multiverse explanation of the Big Bang discussed in chapter 3. I use the word believe here because these scientists have no scientific way of demonstrating their conclusions. In Traynor's case there is evidence, including the medical tests discussed above, and newspaper photos. In the case of atheists their conclusions about miracles and the Big Bang are simply believed through their faith that there is no God. I believe that religious people are on a much sounder footing in dealing with not only miracles but the Big Bang as well, through facts and their faith in God.

One other point should be mentioned. Traynor's cure in not one of the seventy cures at Lourdes that have received official confirmation from the Catholic Church. The problem was not at all with the cure itself but the fact that the paper work for the miracle was not properly submitted.[12]

Healing miracles in general and John Traynor's cure in particular give insight into God's *design imperative*. In such miracles God intervenes in a dramatic way to demonstrate his existence. However, God's intervention is very rare since if healing were common, then we could simply count on God to provide a solution for many if not all illnesses. As a result, our freedom to deal with life would be compromised.

---

12. Apostoli, *Fátima*, 74.

11

Physical Miracles

IN THIS CHAPTER MIRACLES that involve physical effects that can be studied and verified are discussed. Included are miracles involving image formation (Shroud of Turin, Our Lady of Guadalupe), modern eucharistic miracles, and the Miracle of the Sun at Fátima. This chapter does not attempt to give detailed descriptions of all of the aspects of each miracle discussed. Rather, an overview of each of these miracles is given together with references that can be consulted by the reader for additional, in-depth study.

SHROUD OF TURIN

The Shroud of Turin, which consists of linen approximately 14.25 ft long by 3.58 ft wide, is probably the most studied relic in history. Catholic Straight Answers gives an excellent history of the Shroud as well as a discussion of scientific studies on it.[1] Numerous scientific papers have been written on the Shroud, and Shroud papers continue to be published today.

The Shroud has a straw color and it has a faint image of a crucified man on it. Many people believe the image is that of Christ. Many scientists who have studied the Shroud believe that the image was formed by a miraculous burst of radiation energy at the time of Christ's resurrection. Figure 11.1a shows a black and white photograph of the frontal image on the Shroud.

---

1. "What Is Shroud."

Physical Miracles

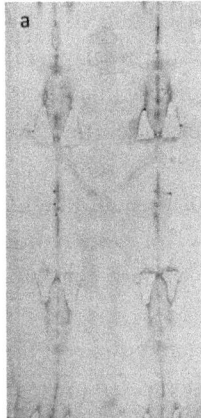

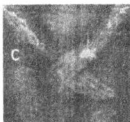

Figure 11.1. Positive(a) and Negative(b) Images of Shroud of Turin and Blow Up of Hand Area(c)[2]

There is also a dorsal (back) image on the Shroud. The Shroud was in a fire in 1532 and the fire caused the triangular holes shown in Figure 11.1a and b. The fire did not damage the image itself.

In 1898 an Italian photographer, Secondo Pia, photographed the Shroud and he made a remarkable discovery. Unlike digital cameras today, Pia's photography used photographic film that resulted in negatives from which prints of the object photographed could be made. When Pia looked at one of his photographic negatives he discovered that the Shroud itself acted like a photographic negative! Figure 11.1b shows a photographic negative image of the Shroud. The difference in the details that can be seen between Figures 11.1a and 11.1b is remarkable.

In 1978 a team of 33 scientists carried out extensive studies on the Shroud. The project was called the Shroud of Turin Research Project, abbreviated STURP.[3] A report from STURP was issued in 1981 and many papers from the project were published. Two key results from STURP's work were that the image on the Shroud definitely was not painted, and that the Shroud contained real human blood.

How the image on the Shroud was formed remained a mystery, and even today it is still a mystery. Interestingly, even though the Shroud acts like a photographic negative, the blood marks do not act as negatives. The wrist wound in Figure 11.1a shows up dark, as blood would. In Figures 11.1b,

2. "Photos," #93 section 2G, and #199 section 7E.
3. "STURP."

and 11.1c the wrist blood shows up light. So, even though the image on the Shroud acts like a photographic negative, the blood acts like it is positive from a photography point of view. From this result researchers conclude that the blood was transferred to the Shroud before the image was formed.

In addition to its remarkable photographic properties, the medical facts that can be learned from the Shroud are equally remarkable. Figure 1c shows a blow up of the hands in Figure 11.1b. The nail wounds in most crucifixes go through the palm of Christ's hands. However, in order to support a body's weight, the nails would have to go through the wrists, just as shown in Figure 11.1c.

As can be seen in Figure 11.1c no thumbs are visible on the Shroud. When a nail goes through the wrist it damages the median nerve and causes the thumb to retract. As a result, the thumbs would retract toward the palms and not be seen. The medical details that can be learned from the Shroud are completely consistent with the crucifixion details given in the four Gospels.

In the short summary given here it is not possible to cover all of the many facts that support the authenticity of Shroud. In addition to all the scientific facts presented by STURP, numismatic studies, botany studies, fabric studies, and historical facts all support the Shroud's authenticity. The one negative fact that has been reported involves radiocarbon dating, which was carried out in 1988.[4]

Radiocarbon dating estimates the age of a sample by measuring the concentration of radioactive carbon 14 (labeled ^{14}C below) in it. Three laboratories carried out radiocarbon dating of the Shroud, and the results of this dating gave a range of AD 1260 to 1390 for the age, indicating that the Shroud was a medieval cloth. If these dates are valid, a super forger would have had medical knowledge that was not available in medieval times. Further, a super forger would have had to use a methodology to produce the image that cannot be duplicated today, even with all the scientific knowledge available. Also, why would a medieval forger make an image that was a photographic negative, centuries before photography was invented?

The statistical analysis of the ^{14}C data given in the 1988 radiocarbon dating study was subsequently questioned by van Haelst[5] who showed that the data contained a systematic bias. The portion of the Shroud tested was approximately 1.5 inches long by ¾ inch wide and yet the ^{14}C dates differed by over two hundred years from one end of the test sample to the other.

4. Damon, "Nature," 611–15.
5. van Haelst, "Radiocarbon."

Physical Miracles

All the ¹⁴C dates should have been close to one another. There was a trend in the data, since ¹⁴C age decreased from the bottom of the Shroud sample toward its top. The top was closer to the center of the Shroud.

Casabianca and co-workers recently carried out a thorough, rigorous statistical analysis of the raw data that were measured during the 1988 ¹⁴C dating study. Interestingly, it took a court order for this data to be released in 2017 (twenty-nine years after it was available) by the owner of the data, the British Museum. Casabianca and co-workers conclude:

> The discussed statistical analysis reinforced the argument against the goodness of the radiocarbon dating of the TS, suggesting the presence of serious incongruities among the raw measurements. Our results, which are compatible with those previously reported by many other authors . . . strongly suggest that homogeneity is lacking in the data. The measurements made by the three laboratories on the TS sample suffer from a lack of precision which seriously affects the reliability of the 95% AD 1260–390 interval.[6]

In short, the statistical analysis given in the 1988 radiocarbon dating study was faulty as was the conclusion of a medieval date for the Shroud's production. *The proper conclusion should have been that the trend in the data did not allow for a statistically significant determination of the Shroud's age.*

Professor Giulio Fanti and co-workers have recently published results[7, 8] on four methods of measuring the age of linen samples. These authors first developed a calibration model for each method by applying it to a number of linen samples of various ages. Then they applied each method to a sample from the Shroud and used the calibration models to estimate the Shroud's age.

The methods studied were: light scattering (method-1) and x-ray scattering (method-2), light absorption (method-3), and mechanical strength testing (method-4). Fanti and co-workers Shroud dating results are: light scattering → 200 BC ± 500 yrs, x-ray-scattering → first century AD, light absorption → 300 BC ± 400 yrs, and mechanical testing → 372 AD ± 400 yrs. All four methods date the Shroud to Christ's time. As a result of Fanti's research and the faulty statistical analysis given in the 1988 radiocarbon dating study, it can be concluded that the medieval dating of the Shroud is not valid.

6. Casabianca, "Archaeometry," 1223–31.
7. Fanti, *Shroud*, chap. 5, 6.
8. Caro, "Heritage," 860–70.

God the Geometer

Today science does not have an explanation for how the image on the Shroud was formed. Over the years several ideas have been proposed for the image formation mechanism that attempt to explain the image's unique characteristics. For example, the Shroud's image has three dimensional properties. Today, the Shroud's image formation is the subject of active research.

At present the best image formation hypothesis is that at the time of the resurrection there was a burst of radiation energy that took place from the body wrapped in the Shroud, and this energy produced the image. This process would be similar to what is described in the Gospels as happening during Christ's Transfiguration: "Six days later, Jesus took Peter, James, and John, the brother of James, up on a high mountain by themselves. While they watched, Jesus' appearance was changed; his face became bright like the Sun, and his clothes became white as light" (Matt 17:1–2). If the image was produced by radiation emanating from Christ's body, it was the result of a miracle.

Recently Professor Giulio Fanti has published an article[9, 10] and a co-authored book with Robert Siefker[11] on a very interesting and promising radiation hypothesis about how the Shroud's image was formed. Fanti's hypothesis is based on a phenomenon, called the Holy Fire, that occurs at the Church of the Holy Sepulchre in Jerusalem. The church was built in the fourth century over Christ's tomb. Since then, essentially every year the Holy Fire has occurred in the church on the Orthodox Holy Saturday.[12] Skarlakisis has described seventy witnesses to the Holy Fire from the fourth century to the present time.[13] Both he and Fanti show photographs of the phenomenon in their books, and there are videos of it on the web. Around 2 PM the Holy Fire appears and it spontaneously lights a bundle of candles held by an Orthodox Patriarch. The fire is then transferred to people waiting outside the Edicule, which contains Christ's tomb.

In 2008 a Russian physicist, Andrey Volkov carried out electromagnetic radiation measurements on the Holy Fire at the time of its appearance. Volkov published the results of his research in 2012 and Fanti and Siefker quote Volkov as follows:

9. Fanti, "Holy Fire and Body."

10. This article is available without cost from Heritage Journal (https://www.mdpi.com/journal/heritage).

11. Fanti, *Holy Fire and Divine*.

12. The date for Orthodox Easter Saturday differs from that for Western Easter Saturday since it is based on the Julian calendar not the Gregorian calendar.

13. Skarlakadis, *Holy Fire*.

Physical Miracles

the appearance of Light is an inseparable part of all these incredible, inexplicable phenomena that have the same electrical nature.

1. The inexplicable appearance of plasma, which, according to him [Volkov], is a miracle itself.
2. Inexplicable and unreasonable electric charge of the air in combination with a powerful difference in electric potentials.
3. The appearance of an electric discharge at the moment of the Holy Light descending.

Volkov added that the Holy Light is accompanied by an appearance of plasma, which looks very similar to a low-temperature [cold] plasma.[14]

Since the Holy Fire involves a cold plasma, the candles that are lit from it initially do not burn as evidenced by a photo that Professor Fanti took when he studied the Holy Fire in 2019. He held a bunch of candles that were lit by the Holy Fire and had the photo shown in Figure 11.2 taken.

Figure 11.2 Professor Fanti with Holy Fire in 2019.[15]

---

14. Fanti, *Holy Fire and Divine*, 177.
15. Fanti, "Holy Fire and Body," 106.

Amazingly, the flame does not burn or cause any pain to Professor Fanti's face. After ten to fifteen minutes the temperature of a candle lit from the Holy Fire increases toward that of a candle burning with an ordinary flame.

Fanti has listed twenty-four characteristics of the Shroud and its image and he discussed the various hypotheses that have been proposed to explain the image.[16] His hypothesis, which he calls, *Divine Photography*, potentially can explain all twenty-four characteristics, while the other hypotheses he discusses cannot. From what Professor Fanti observed and measured in 2019, Fanti and Siefker conclude that the Holy Fire is miraculous.[17]

One objection that had been raised to the Holy Fire involves the fact that after the Orthodox Patriarch enters the Edicule, its door is closed. Since he cannot be seen, the question about whether he has some hidden source of ignition has been raised. Three answers to this objection can be given. First, as Skarlakisis has stated, prior to 1483 the door of the Edicule was open for viewing. The vast majority of the seventy witnesses, of several different faiths, he discusses testified before 1483 and reported seeing the appearance of the Holy Fire.[18] Secondly, although a cold plasma can be created in a laboratory with sophisticated equipment, there is no known way it could be created in a church.[19] Lastly, the Patriarch is searched prior to entering the Edicule.

All Shroud researchers agree that additional research on the cloth is necessary to answer the many questions that have been raised about it. Further, additional research on the Holy Fire should be conducted. Whether the authorities, who could authorize this research, would agree is another question.

OUR LADY OF GUADALUPE

The Knights of Columbus (K of C) have a special devotion to and reverence for Our Lady of Guadalupe. The description below is taken from a writeup on the K of C website and reprinted with their permission.[20] On Saturday, December 9, 1531, while on his way for religious instruction in Mexico City, Juan Diego, an Indian and recent convert to Christianity, heard

16. Fanti, "Holy Fire and Body," 109–10.
17. Fanti, *Holy Fire and Divine*, 309.
18. Skarlakadis, *Holy Fire*, 26.
19. Fanti, *Holy Fire and Divine*, 124, 195–96.
20. "Our Lady."

Physical Miracles

singing coming from the top of Tepeyac hill. Suddenly, the singing stopped, and a woman's voice called out to him: Juan. Ascending the hill, Juan Diego found himself before a beautiful woman adorned in clothing that shone like the Sun.

The woman introduced herself as the Immaculate Mother of God and explained the reason for her appearance: she came to request a church to be built there, and she wanted Juan Diego to take her request to the head of the church in Mexico, Bishop Juan de Zumárraga. The task would not be easy. Like many New World missionaries, Friar Zumárraga was suspicious of supposed visionaries, fearing it was indigenous idolatry. Skeptical of Juan Diego and the Virgin's message, the bishop sent him away, but promised to listen again at a later time.

Dejected, Juan Diego returned to the Virgin and begged her to send someone more esteemed than himself. The Virgin listened tenderly but responded firmly, insisting that Juan Diego be her messenger. The following day (December 10th), Juan Diego returned to the bishop and recounted the many details of the apparition. This time, the bishop requested that Juan Diego return with evidence of the miraculous appearance.

To be sure Juan Diego was being honest, the bishop sent two men to follow him. But after trailing Juan Diego for some time, the men lost sight of him, and told the bishop that Juan Diego was a fraud deserving punishment. Meanwhile, Juan Diego arrived at Tepeyac hill and told the Virgin of the bishop's request; she in turn asked Juan Diego to come back the following day, when she would give him the requested sign for the bishop.

Returning home, Juan Diego was met with sad news: his uncle Juan Bernardino had become deathly ill. Instead of going to Tepeyac hill, the next day (December 11th) Juan Diego found a doctor, but nothing could be done. So, on Monday, December 12, Juan Diego put on his tilma (cloak) for warmth and went to find a priest. Hoping to avoid any delays, he took a different path so as to avoid the Virgin.

But as he neared Tepeyac, she descended from the hill, asking what was wrong. She then reassured the sorrowful Juan Diego by declaring her motherhood and promising that his uncle was already healed. Hearing this, Juan Diego asked for the sign for the bishop, and went to the hilltop as she instructed him. There in this barren, wintery spot, he found a garden of sweet-smelling flowers; he picked the flowers and brought them back down to the Virgin, who arranged them in his tilma. Juan Diego then set out for the bishop's house.

When Juan Diego arrived, the servants refused him entry, but eventually let him enter when they could not take the flowers from his tilma. Before the bishop, Juan Diego recounted the Virgin's words and the miracle of the flowers. When Juan Diego opened his tilma and flowers fell out, an even greater miracle was revealed: on the tilma's surface was the Virgin's image. The bishop and those in the room fell to their knees, admiring and praying, and the bishop asked to be shown the place for the Virgin's church.

With his mission fulfilled, Juan Diego returned home to find his uncle completely healed, just as the Virgin had promised. Even more, the Virgin had appeared to Juan Bernardino, too, and had told him her name: "the Perfect Virgin Holy Mary of Guadalupe." Two weeks later, the day after Christmas, her chapel was completed, and the tilma with its image was placed above the altar.

In 1974 the Guadalupe Basilica was built on Tepeyac hill. Figure 11.3 gives a photo of Juan Diego's original tilma which today hangs above the high altar of the Guadalupe Basilica on Tepeyac hill.

Figure 11.3. Juan Diego's Original Tilma[21]

21. "Image."

Physical Miracles

Catholic News World gives seven scientific facts about the image on Juan Diego's tilma. Here I list only two of the facts:

> The image shows no sign of deterioration after nearly 500 years! The tilma or cloak of Juan Diego on which the image of Our Lady has been imprinted, is a coarse fabric made from the threads of the maguey cactus. This fiber [usually] disintegrates within 20–60 years. There is no under sketch, no sizing and no protective over-varnish on the image; Studies have not succeeded in discovering the origin of the coloration of the Image. In 1979, Americans Philip Callahan and Jody B. Smith studied the image with infrared rays [light] and discovered to their surprise that there was no trace of paint and that the fabric had not been treated with any kind of technique.[22]

The Magis Center agrees with Callahan and Smith's conclusions but points out that:

> There are several parts of the cloth which have been painted on some time after the original image was created. These parts include the moon underneath the Virgin's feet, the angel holding the cloth, and the rays coming from the image. The original image of the Virgin herself, however, does not appear to have been painted by an artist. There is no sketch underneath it, no brush strokes, and no corrections. It appears to have been produced in a single step.[23]

The K of C has published a beautiful color image of Our Lady of Guadalupe. Around the sides of this image eighteen facts about it are discussed in detail. The image has characteristics that appealed to the native Aztec people. For example: "the coloring of her [Mary's] face indicates that she a mestizo (of mixed race), indicating that she belongs to both the Spaniards and the natives, and thus all people."[24] After Mary's miraculous appearance vast numbers of the natives renounced their idols, superstitions, human sacrifices, and polygamy, and asked to be baptized. Nine years after the apparitions, *nine million* natives had converted to the Christian faith.

---

22. "Science behind," para. 3, 7.
23. "Science or Lack," para 5,6.
24. "Secrets," Her Face.

MODERN EUCHARISTIC MIRACLES

On Nov. 3, 2021 Jeanette Williams published an article on the Ascension Press website entitled: "The Amazing Science of Recent Eucharistic Miracles: A Message from Heaven?"[25] In her article, Jeanette points out that more than one hundred eucharistic miracles have been reported since the earliest days of the church to the present.

Here I discuss five examples of modern eucharistic miracles that she discusses, since they are all backed by scientific evidence. Complete details of the modern eucharistic miracles are given in references cited with each. These references also discuss the scientific measurements that were made to corroborate each miracle and they give photos of the Hosts involved in the miracles. The discussion below is a very slightly modified version of what was in Jeanette's article and it is published here with the permission of Ascension Press. The five modern eucharistic miracles she discusses are:

- *1992 and 1996, Buenos Aires, Argentina*: In 1992, consecrated particles left on the corporal were put into water to dissolve and locked in the tabernacle, as the church prescribes for disposing of consecrated Hosts. One week later, they had changed into a red substance. Then again in 1996 after a consecrated Host fell to the ground and was also put in water to dissolve, it was found a few days later to have turned into a bloody substance. Both cases were sent to be tested by the archbishop of Buenos Aires, who was none other than our current Pope Francis.[26]

- *2006, Tixtla, Mexico*: During a retreat, a religious sister who was distributing Communion looked down and noticed that one of the Hosts had begun to bleed and transform.[27]

- *2008, Sokolka, Poland*: A consecrated Host fell to the ground during Communion and was put in water and locked in a tabernacle to dissolve. A week later, most of the Host was dissolved except for a red "clot" that remained.[28]

---

25. Williams, "Amazing."
26. "Eucharistic Buenos."
27. "Eucharistic Tixla."
28. "Eucharistic Sokolka."

- *2013, Legnica, Poland*: A consecrated Host fell and was put in water and locked in a tabernacle. Two weeks later a red spot covered one-fifth of the undissolved Host.[29]

Each of these occurrences received intensive study with highly advanced technology. In several cases, doctors did not know the source of the material. And yet, in all the cases, the same results were found:

- The blood is human, AB blood type; human DNA was found; white blood cells, red blood cells, hemoglobin, and macrophages were present, indicating fresh blood; in the Tixtla miracle, the blood clearly emanated from within, because the blood on the surface had begun to coagulate but the interior blood was still fresh, as with a bleeding wound.
- The flesh is human myocardium tissue of the left ventricle of an inflamed heart; in the miracles from Argentina and Poland, there was evidence of trauma from the presence of thrombi, indicating repeated lack of oxygen; lesions present showed rapid cardiac spasms typical in the final phases of death.
- In the Sokolka miracle, the remaining Host is tightly interconnected with the fibers of human tissue, penetrating each other inseparably, as if the bread were transforming into flesh. "Even NASA scientists, who have at their disposal the most modern analytical techniques, would not be able to artificially recreate such a thing," affirmed Dr. Sobaniec-Lotowska, one of the examining experts.

Dr. Frederick Zugibe, a forensic doctor at Columbia University who examined the Argentinian miracle, did not know the source of the sample and told the doctor who brought it to him, "If white blood cells were present (in the heart tissue), it is because at the moment you brought me the sample, it was pulsating." When he learned the source of the sample, he was shocked and deeply moved.

In her article Jeanette asks why has the Lord suddenly multiplied eucharistic miracles in the last few decades? Are we, like Doubting Thomas, refusing to believe unless we see, touch, and feel for ourselves? Jesus in his love for Thomas condescended to let him see, touch, and feel his wounds in order to believe.

29. "Eucharistic Legnica."

Perhaps he is now doing the same for us. So many young people have rejected religion as unscientific. So, here's the science to prove our faith. Others say they don't believe in religion because it's just opinion or contrary to reason. The five eucharistic miracles discussed by Jeanette Williams provide quantifiable, measurable, physical evidence for the occurrence supernatural events.

MIRACLE AT FÁTIMA

Father Andrew Apostoli wrote the excellent book, *Fátima For Today: The Urgent Marian Message of Hope*, and it thoroughly documents the Miracle at Fátima.[30] In 1917 Fátima was a small village in Portugal. Starting on May 13, 1917 the Virgin Mary appeared as a beautiful young woman to three children from a nearby hamlet, Lucia dos Santos, Francisco Marto, and Jacinto Marto. Lucia was ten years old, Francisco almost eight years old, and Jacinta was seven years old. Mary appeared above a holmoak tree while the children were tending sheep at nearby Cova da Iria. In the first apparition the children saw a beautiful woman dressed in white, but they did not know her identity.

At the time World War I was raging and the woman told the children that if a message of prayer was spread then world peace would result. Interestingly, although all three children saw the woman, only Lucia and Jacinta heard her speak. The woman told the children that she would return on the 13th of the month for a total of six months at the same hour. The woman also told the children they will need to sacrifice and suffer, but that they will end up in heaven. She told the children to say the rosary every day to bring about peace and to devote themselves to the Immaculate Heart of Mary.[31]

Word leaked out in Fátima about the apparition and as a result when the children went to Cova da Iria on June 13, they were accompanied by about fifty people.[32] The woman repeated her request to the children to say the Rosary every day in order to keep world peace. By the time of the third apparition on July 13, word had spread throughout Portugal. There were now about four thousand people present.[33] The woman revealed three secrets to the children; she showed the children that hell is a horrible place; she

30. Apostoli, *Fátima*.
31. Apostoli, *Fátima*, 45.
32. Apostoli, *Fátima*, 51.
33. Apostoli, *Fátima*, 56–57.

Physical Miracles

predicted World War II and the persecution of Christians in Russia; and she said that there will be additional persecution of Christians. The woman also told the children that she would reveal her identity on October 13.

Before August 13, the three children were imprisoned by the police, who believed they were making up the apparitions. They wanted the children to admit that it was all a hoax. The children stood firm and were subsequently released. On August 19, the woman appeared again and told the children to pray for sinners. On September 13, the crowd at Cova da Iria numbered about twenty-five thousand.[34] As a result, the children had difficulty getting to the holmoak tree. During this apparition the woman promised that the children would see a miracle during her appearance on October 13.

The sixth and final apparition occurred on October 13, 1917. "Estimates of the crowd ranged from forty to eighty thousand at the Cova itself. Another twenty thousand were watching from about twenty-five miles around."[35] The woman revealed her identity as the Lady of the Rosary and she requested that a chapel be built on the spot. After dialoging with Lucia, Our Lady made the children reflect on the Sun.

Then, the Miracle of the Sun happened. This miracle has been described as:

> According to various witness accounts, the rainy sky cleared up, and the ground that was wet from the rain became dry. The Sun appeared 'dancing around' and 'zig-zagging' in the sky within broken clouds, giving it the name of the Miracle of the Sun. Some say that the dancing Sun even appeared to fly closer to the Earth and then jump back into its place quickly. Others also mentioned multicolored light and radiant colors all over the sky. They said the Miracle of the Sun lasted for at least ten minutes. The children were then finally believed by the people of Fátima.[36]

The crowd was both terrified and in awe with what they saw.

In his book Father Apostoli has three photos of the crowds watching the Miracle of the Sun and two of the photos are from the front page of the newspaper *O Século* that reported on it. Shown below in Figure 11.4 is one photo from *O Século* taken by Judah Ruah in 1917 that shows people

---

34. Apostoli, *Fátima*, 108.
35. Apostoli, *Fátima*, 120–21.
36. Silva, "What," The Final Apparition, para. 2.

watching the miracle.[37] Confirmations of the miracle from members of the crowd appeared in newspapers along with photos of the miracle.

Figure 11.4. Crowd Watching the Miracle of the Sun October 13, 1917.

The physical facts that can be used to scientifically study the miracles discussed in this chapter are as follows. First, both the Shroud of Turin and the tilma of Guadalupe can be seen today. The Shroud is probably the most widely studied relic in history. The tilma has not been studied as much but studies of both images attest to their authenticity. The five modern eucharistic miracles have been studied in depth and photographs of them are available. Lastly, there are photos of the Fátima miracle as well as newspaper stories on it that can be consulted. There is no question that all these miracles actually took place.

The discussions in this chapter have been kept short so that all the miracles could be covered. The reader is encouraged to look into the citations on each provided in the bibliography to study them in more detail.

The fact that miracles are rare gives insight into God's *design imperative* for our universe. If miracles were common then our freedom to solve life's problems would be compromised. God intervenes in ways that can be seen and studied scientifically but at a rate that does not compromise our freedom. In this regard the question raised by Jeanette Williams about why the frequency of eucharistic miracles though small, is increasing in recent times is interesting. Have humans become, in Jeanette's words, "Doubting Thomases"?

37. Ruah, "Miracle."

12

Conclusions

IN CHAPTER 1 DESIGN of the universe is discussed from an engineering perspective and a definition of design is given as follows. According to the text *Mechanical Engineering Design*, a *design imperative* is the requirement to: "Design (subject to *problem-solving constraints*) a component, system, or process that will perform a specified task (subject to certain *solution constraints*) optimally."[1] The specified task is the *objective* or goal of the design and the parenthetical expressions refer to qualifications placed on the design. The *problem-solving constraints* involve what the designer knows or is able to do. The *solution constraints* involve issues like the design's functionality, safety, reliability, and conformity to standards and legal codes.

Now consider the design of our universe. In this design, God had to have an *objective* in mind, and there were *solution constraints* that had to be met. Since an all-knowledgeable God carried out the design there would be no *problem-solving constraints* in the *design imperative*. The *design imperative* and the *solution constraints* lead to tradeoffs in the final universe. Just what were the *objective* and the *solution constraints* in this design?

Throughout the book various insights into God's *design imperative* for the universe have been highlighted. These insights are consistent with the following answers to the question of what God's *objective* was and what the *solution constraints* were in the design of our universe:

---

1. Shigley, *Mechanical*, 5.

God the Geometer

- The design *objective* was to create a universe where intelligent life that is truly free could evolve.

- The *solution constraints* were that the design was a physical design with all its inherent limitations; the design was also an *autonomous design* where God did not choose to regularly intervene in his universe; and God wanted humans to be able to use their intelligence to see him as the Creator of our universe.

The most important indicator of the design *objective* involves the question of how free will can be possible in a physical universe? Quantum indeterminacy, discussed in chapter 8, was a truly remarkable and ingenious way for God to answer this question. On a macroscopic scale our universe acts in essentially a deterministic, i.e. non-probabilistic, manner. For example, we can see a table and know its exact location and that it is not moving. But, on a microscopic scale probability reigns, so that the future cannot be predicted with 100 percent certainty.

We can never know the exact location and velocity of very small particles. As discussed in chapter 8, microscopic probabilistic events can have macroscopic effects. As a result of this aspect of the *design imperative*, humans have free will to shape the world around them. Humans have the ability to choose between good and evil and their choice changes the world in which we live, and determines its future.

One can ask why God used an *autonomous design* for our universe? If God regularly intervened in our universe to solve problems, then his presence would be obvious. Such a situation would create problems for humans using their free will. As discussed in chapter 9 being free requires something to be free about. If God regularly solved problems, that approach would deprive humans of their freedom to try to solve the same problems.

Another issue with God's presence being too obvious involves his awesome power. In chapter 2 the truly unbelievable energy associated with the Big Bang is discussed. If God's presence in our universe were obvious then humans could easily be intimidated by God's power and might compared to their own. It would be difficult for humans to exercise free will in such a case.

Similarly, if it were possible to definitively prove God's existence, for example using science, such a proof would also result in the elimination of free will. In such a case one would not be free to either accept or reject God, since his existence would be absolutely certain. Although science supports

Conclusions

faith, faith is required to bridge the gap that must exist between science and proof of God's existence.

John Haught is a theologian and a Distinguished Research Professor at Georgetown University. He has published a number of books on faith and science. In *God After Darwin,* Haught explains why he thinks God acts as he does:

> Indeed, an infinite love must in some sense 'absent' or 'restrain' itself, precisely in order to give the world the 'space' in which to become something distinct from the creative love that constitutes 'other.' We should anticipate, therefore, that any universe rooted in an unbounded love would have some features that appear to us as random or undirected.[2]

Haught's view of God's relationship to humans is that he gives us the space we need to express our free will and thereby live rewarding lives.

An *autonomous design* camouflages God's presence in the universe, but humans can use their intellect to see his presence. Humans have been able to understand the fine-tuning of our universe and our solar system, discussed in chapters 3 and 4. As discussed in chapters 5 and 6, humans have been able to see patterns in evolution and to understand that chance plays a role. As discussed in chapter 9, what has been described as natural evil can be understood as being the result of tradeoffs resulting from the *design imperative* of our universe. Lastly as discussed in chapters 10 and 11, investigation of miracles not only validates the miracles, but it also demonstrates God's presence in our world. So, one way humans have discovered God is through the use of their intelligence.

One way science can support and enhance faith is through incorporating scientific knowledge into theology. In *Deeper Than Darwin,* John Haught points out that most of the world's religions have yet to integrate the knowledge gained by modern science into their theology. He writes:

> The world's religions, at least during the period of their emergence, knew nothing about Big Bang cosmology, deep time or biological evolution. Generally speaking, they have still not caught up with these ideas. Even in the scientific West, the findings of evolutionary biology and cosmology continue to lurk only at the fringes of contemporary theological awareness.[3]

---

2. Haught, *God*, 112.
3. Haught, *Deeper*, 161.

God the Geometer

On December 31, 2022 Pope Benedict XVI passed away, and after his death his final spiritual testament to the church was published. The pope's spiritual testament has a paragraph on faith and science that lends support to Haught's position on integrating science into faith. Pope Benedict XVI's testament reads:

> What I said before to my countrymen, I now say to all those in the Church who have been entrusted to my service: Stand firm in the faith! Do not let yourselves be confused! It often seems that science—the natural sciences on the one hand and historical research (especially exegesis of Sacred Scripture) on the other—are able to offer irrefutable results at odds with the Catholic faith. I have experienced the transformations of the natural sciences since long ago and have been able to see how, on the contrary, *apparent certainties against the faith have vanished, proving to be not science, but philosophical interpretations* only apparently pertaining to science; just as, on the other hand, it is in dialogue with the natural sciences that faith, too, has learned to understand better the limit of the scope of its claims, and thus its specificity.[4]

In chapter 2 the two creation stories in Genesis were discussed and it was pointed out that neither is scientific. However, it was further pointed out that Genesis states that God created the universe from nothing, ex nihilo. This theological aspect of Genesis is fully supported by the Big Bang. As far as we know, before the Big Bang there was nothing, and then our universe came into being. Our universe had a beginning just as Genesis states. So, in the case of creation science supports faith.

One of the very important aspects of Christianity is the concept of original sin:

> Original sin is the Christian doctrine that holds that humans, through the fact of birth, inherit a tainted nature in need of regeneration and a proclivity to sinful conduct. The biblical basis for the belief is generally found in Genesis 3, the story of the expulsion of Adam and Eve from the Garden of Eden.[5]

St. Augustine (354–430) was the first author to use this phrase. Without original sin there would be no need of redemption, and Christ entering our world.

---

4. Brockhaus, "FULL," para 6.
5. "Original," para. 1.

Conclusions

The Adam and Eve story is clearly not scientific, but it does address the flawed nature that humans possess. Original sin is another important area of faith where science can be supportive. Science can provide a very reasonable explanation for our flawed nature.

Domning and Hellwig have published an incisive book on the origin of original sin entitled *Original Selfishness: Original Sin and Evil in the Light of Evolution*.[6] The book was primarily written by Domning, a paleontologist, and Hellwig, a theologian, commented on what Domning had written. Domning emphasizes that "the evolutionary process necessarily enforces selfish behavior on all living things." The book puts forth the idea that original sin arose from the fact that we evolved from lower life forms where selfishness is an advantage. We still have the conflict between selfishness and true altruism built into our genes.

Two examples can be given for illustration about animal selfishness. Masked boobies in the Galapagos Islands typically lay two eggs, one of which hatches first. If the first hatchling is healthy it is stronger than the second and it pushes the second hatchling out of the nest, resulting in its death and thereby committing siblicide. All of this takes place with the parents watching. It may be that there is only enough food available to feed one hatchling and the second chick is simply insurance that the mating pair will have a survivor.

During the mating season, elephant seals brutally attack one another to keep control of their harem. The goal of these attacks and the hatchling's behavior is maximizing the probability that one's genes are passed on. There is no sense of sharing or altruism in the animal kingdom, and animals' behavior conforms to what Dawkins discusses in *The Selfish Gene*.[7] Animals primarily strive to perpetuate their own genes at the expense of other animals.

Once intelligence evolved not only was cooperation (true altruism) important for survival of humans, but humans also became aware of how their selfish behavior could hurt others. Even so humans still had a built-in tendency to be selfish, that was associated with the life forms from which they evolved. It is the conflict between acting altruistically and selfishly that is at the root of original sin. Thus, one can use science to define original sin as:

---

6. Domning, "Original."
7. Dawkins, *Selfish*, 2.

God the Geometer

Original sin: acting selfishly in spite of knowing the harm that the selfish behavior inflicts on others.

As we evolved mankind was free to move in a direction that increased true altruism in the world. But humans had free will and therefore they could also evolve in a direction that increased suffering in the world. It appears that progressing in either direction could take place faster than the glacial time scale for the evolution of physical traits. Christine Kenneally has published an interesting book, *The Invisible History of the Human Race: How DNA and History Shape Our Identities and Our Futures*, that illustrates this point.

Kenneally discusses an example of how bad behavior toward one generation can affect four to five generations in the future.[8] In the mid-1800s slaves were taken from several countries in Africa. In some cases, family members turned over other family members to the slave traders. As a result, in the countries affected people became very suspicious of one another and they lost trust in others. This suspicious nature was encoded rather quickly into the behavior of the people in the slave trade countries. Well after the slave trade ceased, inhabitants in these countries were still very suspicious of others. Today the countries from which slaves were taken are poorer than neighboring countries that were not affected as much by slave trade. Commerce in the slave trade countries is poor since one requirement for a robust economy is trust in others, which doesn't exist there.

This example indicates that selfish behavior early on in human existence could quickly affect the development of mankind in a negative way. Similarly, had truly altruistic behavior been the norm this could have affected the development of mankind in a positive way. We were free to choose either direction. Looking at early recorded history indicates that mankind made the wrong choice. There are numerous examples that one could give. For example, why would any nation use crucifixion with all its suffering as a means of capital punishment? The fact that selfishness won out over true altruism is the reason that mankind needed redemption.

The goal of this book is to demonstrate that science supports faith. Topics in cosmology, astronomy, evolution and physics have been presented that demonstrate that this support is real. Examining science shows that the statement describing God the Geometer, given at the beginning of this book is correct. "God has created the universe after geometric and harmonic principles, to seek these principles was therefore to seek and

---

8. Kenneally, *Invisible*, 139–46.

Conclusions

worship God."[9] People of faith have nothing to be afraid of when it comes to science. In fact, some of the positions of scientists can be criticized as being untenable, much more that those of believers, e.g. the existence of an unobservable multiverse. Science can also provide a sound basis for theological concepts such as original sin and the creation of the universe. So, it is my hope that the reader can better appreciate how science supports faith, and not be intimidated by scientific advances. The message of the book is that humans should live free and behave altruistically to make the world better place to live.

---

9. "God," Description.

Appendix A

Electromagnetic Force and Radiation

ELECTROMAGNETIC FORCE

THE ELECTROMAGNETIC FORCE IS one of the four fundamental forces in the universe. These forces are electromagnetism, gravity, the weak nuclear force, and the strong nuclear force. We are all familiar with the force of gravity, particularly if we trip and fall, or see an object fall. This appendix gives a brief overview of the electromagnetic force and radiation, which are not quite as familiar as the gravitational force. The weak and strong nuclear forces occur within atomic nuclei and they require some knowledge of physics to be understood. A detailed discussion of them is not necessary for understanding the material in this book.

BYJU'S gives the history of electromagnetism as follows:

> Before the invention of electromagnetism, people or scientists used to think electricity and magnetism are two different topics. The view has changed after James Clerk Maxwell published *A Treatise on Electricity and Magnetism*[1] in the year 1873. The publication states that the interaction of positive and negative charges is mediated by one force. This observation laid a foundation for electromagnetism. Later many scientists like Michael Faraday, Oliver Heaviside, and Heinrich Hertz contributed their ideas in electromagnetism.[2]

1. Maxwell, *Treatise*.
2. "Electromagnetism," para. 3.

Appendix A

The electromagnetic force is a type of physical interaction that occurs between electrically charged particles. The electromagnetic force is the combination of all magnetic and electrical forces between the particles. Charged particles exert an attractive or repulsive force on one another depending on whether each particle is positively or negatively charged. Similarly, magnets repel or attract one another depending on which poles of the magnet, north or south, are brought together. Opposite magnetic poles attract, while the same poles repulse. In both the electrical and magnetic cases, the force exerted is a single force, the electromagnetic force.

The electromagnetic force is used in numerous ways to benefit modern society. For example, electric motors use the electromagnetic force between a magnet and a current carrying coil to produce movement. Electric generators use the electromagnetic force between a magnet and a moving coil to generate electrical energy. Loudspeakers use an electric current flowing through a coil to generate a magnetic field. This field interacts with the field of a permanent magnet to make a diaphragm move and produce sound. In addition to these uses a number of other examples of the use of electromagnetism are given in reference.[3]

No doubt the most important magnetic field with respect to human evolution is the Earth's magnetic field, discussed in chapter 4. This field is shown schematically in Figure A-1.

Figure A-1. Earth's magnetic field.[4]

The curved lines emanating from the Earth indicate the magnetic field produced by rotation of the Earth's molten iron core. The S and N in the figure

3. "Uses," para. 3
4. "Earth's."

Electromagnetic Force and Radiation

indicate south and north poles of the Earth's magnetic field. A compass uses a magnetic needle, and the needle's north pole actually points toward the Earth's south magnetic pole, S, in Figure A-1, because opposite magnetic poles attract. This situation can be a bit confusing since people know compass points to the geographic north. As discussed in chapter 4, without the Earth's magnetic field harmful cosmic rays would strip off the Earth's atmosphere, resulting in a lifeless planet.

RADIATION

The Center for Disease Control has the following discussion on radiation on its website:

> Radiation is energy that comes from a source and travels through space at the speed of light. This energy has an electric field and a magnetic field associated with it, and has wave-like properties. You could also call radiation 'electromagnetic waves'.[5]
>
> - There is a wide range of electromagnetic radiation in nature. Visible light is one example.
> - Radiation with the highest energy includes forms like ultraviolet radiation, x-rays, and gamma rays.
> - X-rays and gamma rays have a lot of energy. When they interact with atoms, they can remove electrons and cause the atom to become ionized.
> - Radiation can damage the DNA in our cells.

Electromagnetic waves have a frequency spectrum shown in Figure A-2 below.

---

5. "What Is Radiation," para. 1.

Appendix A

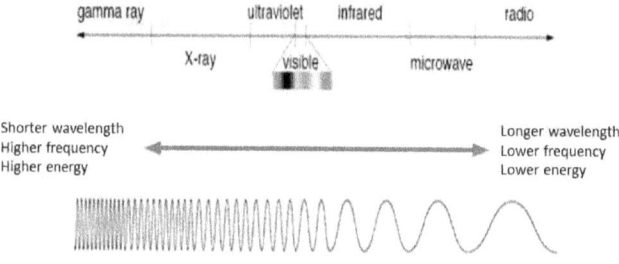

Figure A-2. Electromagnetic spectrum.[6]

The energy content of electromagnetic waves depends on their frequency. The higher frequency waves, e.g. gamma rays and x-rays, oscillate more frequently and they contain more energy than lower frequency waves, e.g. microwave and radio waves. Just after the Big Bang the frequency of the electromagnetic radiation in the universe was unbelievably high, reflecting the energy content of the early universe. Since electromagnetic waves oscillate in both time and space, they produce electric and magnetic fields. A charged particle in the electric field would feel a force from it, and a magnetic particle in the magnetic field would feel a force from it.

Figure A-2 shows that the different types of radiation are all electromagnetic waves that simply have different oscillation frequencies. These different types include: gamma rays, x-rays, ultraviolet, visible light, infrared, microwave, and radio waves.

Various methods of making measurements using electromagnetic waves have been developed. Spectroscopy is the primary tool that has been used to gain information about our universe and solar system. "Spectroscopy is the science of studying materials by measuring their response to different frequencies of radiation. It should be noted that while a few forms of spectroscopy use other forms of radiative energy, such as acoustic or matter waves, spectroscopy is virtually always understood to use electromagnetic radiation to probe matter."[7] The measured response can come from absorption of radiation or scattering of radiation. A discussion of the five basic types of spectroscopy is given by PLATAPUS Technologies.[8] These five

---

6. "Electromagnetic."
7. "Five."
8. "Five."

Electromagnetic Force and Radiation

types are: infrared, ultraviolet-visible, x-ray, nuclear magnetic resonance, and Raman spectroscopy.

Radar is a radiolocation system that uses radio electromagnetic waves to determine the distance (ranging), angle, and radial velocity of objects relative to a site. If an observer is moving relative to an electromagnetic wave or sound wave source, the frequency of the source wave will be shifted when it is measured by the observer. This shift, which can involve either an increase or decrease in frequency, is called the Doppler effect. "Weather radar (also known as Doppler weather radar) is an instrument that sends pulses of electromagnetic energy into the atmosphere to find precipitation, determine its motion and intensity, and identify the precipitation type such as rain, snow or hail."[9] In Doppler radar a storm moves relative to where the Doppler radar is measured.

---

9. "What Is Weather," para. 1.

Appendix B

Proteins

BRITANNICA DEFINES BIOCHEMISTRY AS: "[the] study of the chemical substances and processes that occur in plants, animals, and microorganisms and of the changes they undergo during development and life. It deals with the chemistry of life."[1] Proteins are biochemical molecules that are essential for life. Wikipedia describes proteins as:

> large biomolecules and macromolecules [biopolymers] that comprise one or more long chains of amino acid residues. Proteins perform a vast array of functions within organisms, including catalyzing metabolic reactions, DNA replication, responding to stimuli, providing structure to cells and organisms, and transporting molecules from one location to another. Proteins differ from one another primarily in their sequence of amino acids.[2]

Catalyzing involves accelerating the rate of a chemical reaction. The National Cancer Institute defines metabolic as: "the total of all chemical changes that take place in a cell or an organism to produce energy and basic materials needed for important life processes."[3] DNA and its replication are discussed in chapter 5.

1. "Biochemistry," para. 1.
2. "Protein," para. 1.
3. "Metabolic."

Proteins

Amino acids are the molecules that are the building blocks that combine to form proteins. Figure B-1 shows a schematic diagram of the amino acid glycine.

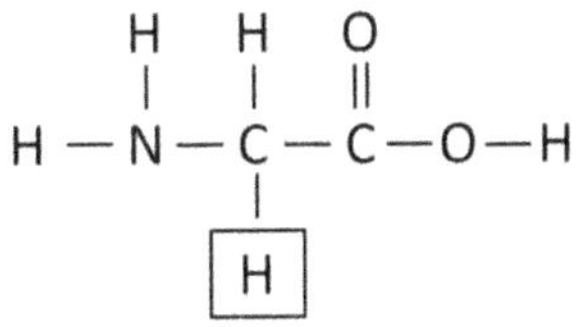

$$\begin{array}{c} \text{H} \quad \text{H} \quad \text{O} \\ | \quad\; | \quad\; \| \\ \text{H}-\text{N}-\text{C}-\text{C}-\text{O}-\text{H} \\ | \\ \boxed{\text{H}} \end{array}$$

Figure B-1. Chemical structure of glycine.

The atoms shown in the diagram are: H = hydrogen, N = nitrogen, C = carbon, and O = oxygen. Each atom forms a different number of bonds with other atoms, shown as straight lines in the diagram. Hydrogen forms one bond, nitrogen forms three bonds, carbon forms four bonds and oxygen forms two bonds. In the case of oxygen in an amino acid, it forms a double bond with the same carbon atom, shown as two parallel lines.

If the hydrogen in the square is replaced with a methyl group, CH3, the resulting amino acid is alanine, shown in Figure B-2.

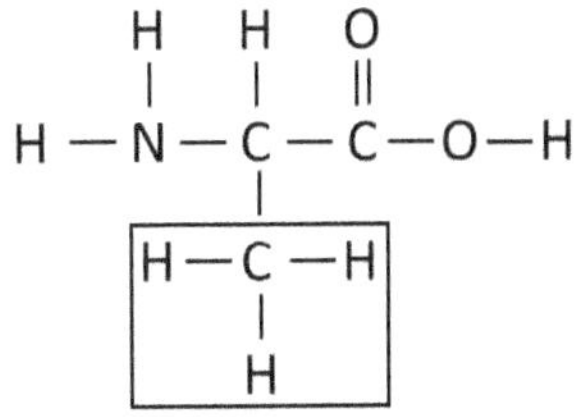

$$\begin{array}{c} \text{H} \quad \text{H} \quad \text{O} \\ | \quad\; | \quad\; \| \\ \text{H}-\text{N}-\text{C}-\text{C}-\text{O}-\text{H} \\ | \\ \boxed{\begin{array}{c} \text{H}-\text{C}-\text{H} \\ | \\ \text{H} \end{array}} \end{array}$$

Figure B-2. Chemical structure of alanine.

In addition to having an H and CH3 bound to the first carbon atom in Figures B-1 and B-2, there are eighteen additional chemical groups that can be bound to the first carbon atom, giving rise to a total of twenty different amino acids in proteins.

To begin to form a protein from amino acids, one of the hydrogen atoms bound to the nitrogen atom reacts with the OH group bound to the second carbon atom to produce water (H2O) and a combination of the two

Appendix B

reacting amino acids. Figure B-3 shows the result of reacting glycine and alanine.

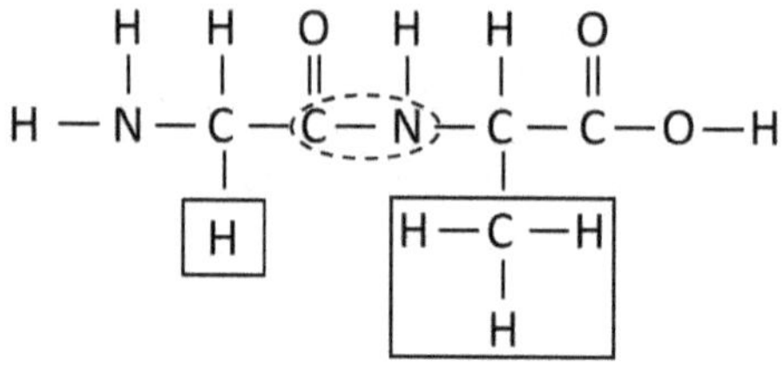

$$\text{H}-\text{N}-\overset{\overset{\text{H}}{|}}{\text{C}}-\overset{\overset{\text{O}}{\|}}{\text{C}}-\overset{\overset{\text{H}}{|}}{\text{N}}-\overset{\overset{\text{H}}{|}}{\underset{\underset{\text{H}}{|}}{\underset{\text{H}-\text{C}-\text{H}}{\text{C}}}}-\overset{\overset{\text{O}}{\|}}{\text{C}}-\text{O}-\text{H}$$

Figure B-3. Peptide bond between glycine and alanine.

The water that is produced is not shown. The carbon nitrogen bond circled in Figure B-3 is called a peptide bond. Note that the structure in Figure B-3 looks similar to an amino acid in that it has two hydrogen atoms attached to a nitrogen atom at its left end and an OH group attached to the carbon that is double bonded to oxygen at its right end. The OH group at the right can be split off and the carbon atom attached to it can form a new peptide bond with the nitrogen atom in one of the twenty amino acids. A water molecule would again be formed as a byproduct. In this manner a long chain of peptide bonds can be formed. The resulting long chain is called a polypeptide chain or peptide backbone for a protein. Proteins are generally between fifty and two thousand amino acids long, all connected with peptide bonds.[4] An exact number of proteins in the human body is unknown, but "most agree that there are around twenty thousand different proteins in our body. Some studies suggest that there might be even more."[5]

In order for proteins to be biologically active and do their job, it is necessary that they be folded properly. As discussed in the chapter 5, proteins typically fold into two different structures, beta-sheets and alpha helices. Protein folding is very complex and a discussion of it can be found in reference.[6]

---

4. "Shape," para. 10.
5. Algren, "What," para. 6.
6. "Proteins Structure."

Appendix C

Genetic Algorithms

CHAPTER 5 GAVE A summary of the theory of evolution, and it is repeated here:

> First, that all organisms produce more offspring than can possibly survive; second, that all organisms within a species vary, one from the other; third, that at least some of this variation is inherited by offspring. From these three facts we infer the principle of natural selection: since only some of the offspring can survive, on average the survivors will be those variants that, by good fortune, are better adapted to changing local environments. Since these offspring will inherit the favorable variations of their parents, organisms of the next generation will, on average, become better adapted to local conditions.[1]

The three rules in the summary involving excess offspring, variation of offspring, and inheritance by offspring can be easily coded into a computer program as an algorithm. Such algorithms have been used to solve complex engineering optimization problems, and they are called genetic algorithms.[2] To illustrate genetic algorithms, I would like to discuss the problem of finding the highest peak in a mountain range, discussed in chapter 6. Although this illustrative problem is simple, it is useful for illuminating the

---

1. Zimmer, *Evolution*, xii.
2. Edgar, *Optimization*, chap. 10.

Appendix C

essential nature and value of genetic algorithms and for showing that they achieve an objective. The example also demonstrates the purposefulness of a genetic algorithm. In order to present important aspects clearly, I will use a simple genetic algorithm, but one which embodies the key characteristics of the methodology. The important attributes of this simple algorithm are the same as those of more complex genetic algorithms, including evolution of life forms.

Figure C-1 illustrates the problem to be addressed, which involves finding the highest peak in a mountain range.

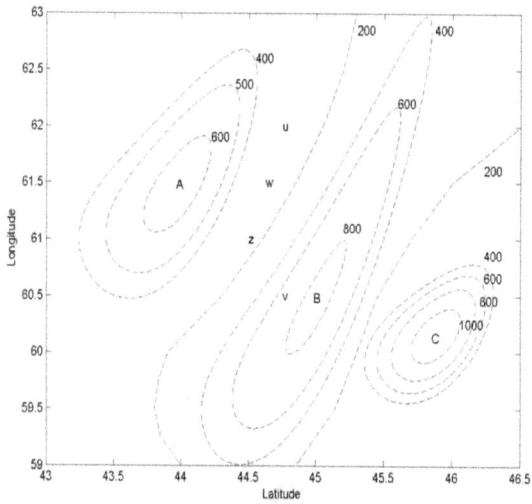

Figure C-1. Topographical map showing peaks.

The x axis is related to the latitude and the y axis to the longitude of a particular location. The dashed topographic curves show points of equal height on the surface of the mountain range to be explored. The numbers to the right of the curves give the height in feet. There are three peaks shown in Figure C-1 and peak C has the maximum altitude, 1,200 feet. The other peaks have heights that are 700 feet for A and 950 feet for B. The starting point for the genetic algorithm is labeled z and it is determined randomly. The height at point z is 225 feet. Since evolution uses only local information, one cannot look out from a location and see where the highest peak is. Doing so would involve using global information. So, imagine that a parent

Genetic Algorithms

who is blindfolded is placed at point z.[3] The reason the parent is blindfolded is that they are not allowed to use their vision to solve the problem. In solving typical optimization problems on a computer, one does not have the ability to use senses like sight, but rather numerical computations only must be used. In addition, the parent's spouse is blindfolded and placed at location u, also determined randomly. The parents will have several offspring, who are also blindfolded, and who are placed at locations which will be determined by the genetic algorithm. Below only two offspring are considered for simplicity. In a real computer application more offspring would be generated.

Next, assume that a binary coding is used for locations. The binary coding is the computer analog of the four chemical bases in DNA, discussed in chapter 5, that nature uses in biological evolution. Using binary coding the starting z and u locations for this example can be written as:

Latitude: z=[0010011010] , u=[0110011010]
Longitude: z=[0001011110] , u=[0000111110]

Consider calculating the latitude at z. It would equal $0*2^{-3} + 0*2^{-2} + 1*2^{-1} \; 0*2^0 + 0*2^1 + 1*2^2 + 1*2^3 + 0*2^4 + 1*2^5 + 0*2^6$ or 44.5.[4] The decimal equivalents of the latitude and longitude for z and u are (44.5, 61) and (44.75, 62) respectively. The locations of the offspring are determined by a combination of the locations of the two parents. For example, one could use the average latitude and longitude of the parents to give the initial location of offspring as:

Latitude: [1010011010], or (44.625)
Longitude: [0011011110], or (61.5)

Next, it is assumed that mutations occur in the offspring, and their genes are almost the same as the average genes inherited from the parents, but in a few locations ones have been replaced with zeros and vice versa. The number of locations where changes are made and the locations

---

3. A real person is not used. Parent is the name of a location on the topographical map. The genetic algorithm can best be explained by using some terms that would apply to a real person, e.g. parent, blindfolded. In the algorithm a parent and an offspring, or two offspring can interact to produce the next generation. This would not occur with humans.

4. The genetic algorithm illustrated uses only ten powers of 2 for simplicity. A real computer application of a genetic algorithm would have many more powers of 2 and a higher resolution.

Appendix C

themselves are chosen at random. Thus, the first two offspring might look like the following:

Latitude: w=[1010011010] , v=[0110011010]
Longitude: w=[0011011110] , v=[0010 011110]

The decimal equivalents for w and v are (44.625, 61.5), and (44.75, 60.5) respectively. The location for the first offspring, w, has not been changed (no mutation), while that for the second offspring, v, has changed significantly (substantial mutation). Two genes in the latitude and one in the longitude, shown in italics, have been changed. Note that in this example offspring w has traits (genes) that are a perfect average of those of the two parents. Offspring v on the other hand has traits that are quite different, which is a not too uncommon situation with real children.

The offspring are now blindfolded and sent to the location given by their genetic code. Assume that at all locations it is possible to measure altitude. Altitude in this example is the objective, which is to be maximized. In evolution the objective is survival. The two parents know their altitude, as do all of the offspring. Everyone reports their altitude and the two people located at the highest altitudes are retained for the next iteration of the algorithm. For Figure C-1 the altitudes of the four people are: z=225, w=290, u=250, and v=640. Thus, w and v would be retained in the algorithm and z and u no longer used. The process is repeated and a new set of offspring is generated, and their altitudes evaluated. If the mutations used are rich enough, and if the process is carried out through many cycles, the two people retained at the end of many cycles eventually wind up at the highest peak, namely point C. It is important to note that in determining the optimum only local information about the altitude has been used, since each participant is blindfolded and unable to see the peaks around them. This process replicates what happens in biological evolution where information that is local is used. Evolution does not go forward based on knowledge or prediction of the future, but rather it uses only current, local conditions.

One can re-run the hill climbing genetic algorithm as many times as desired and each time the result will be peak C. When the algorithm is re-run the path and calculation time to peak C will be different for each run due to the random nature of the mutation process in the algorithm. However, the final result will be the same.

As pointed out in chapter 5, evolution is not random, but it follows patterns, so in this regard evolution differs somewhat from the simple

Genetic Algorithms

algorithm discussed here. One could easily adjust the algorithm to make it closer to evolution by finding out which binary numbers have the largest effect on the objective. Then changes in these numbers could be emphasized over changes in less sensitive numbers.

This simple genetic algorithm satisfies the three rules laid down by Darwin. At most only two of the offspring survive after each cycle,[5] the offspring vary from one another, and the offspring inherit characteristics from their parents. It can be noted that much more sophisticated versions of genetic algorithms than the simple one discussed here are available.[6]

The results from the genetic algorithm can be compared with those achieved by another optimization algorithm, called steepest ascent. With steepest ascent a blindfolded person would measure the altitude in the vicinity of the starting location. For example, they could walk in a small circle centered at their starting point and make a series of measurements as they walked. Then they would move to the highest point on the circle, and repeat the process.

Assume that the first set of circular measurements has its high point in the direction of peak B. With steepest ascent one would start moving towards peak B. Each time a new circular measurement was taken one would move closer to peak B. As one approached peak B there would be no mechanism in the steepest ascent algorithm to back away from peak B and find an even better result. Peak B is locally the highest point around, but it is not the global optimum, which is peak C. The steepest ascent algorithm does not have the ability to get around peak B and find peak C.

Through inheritance from the parents, called crossing over, and mutation, genetic algorithms have the ability to find a global optimum. Although they only use local information genetic algorithms are able to get across valleys and find the peak with the maximum altitude. Genetic algorithms do not get stuck at local optima, as the steepest descent and other algorithms do.

For optimization problems where there are many local optima, this ability to find a global answer is an extremely valuable attribute. Genetic algorithms, however, are typically slow since they require time to achieve their results and that is the reason other approaches to global optimization are used in engineering practice today.

---

5. One or both parents might be at the two highest locations, in which case the parent or parents are retained.

6. Edgar, *Optimization*, chap. 10.

Glossary[1]

Algorithm: a set of instructions that must be followed to solve a problem. Typically, a computer performs calculations based on the instructions.

Altruism: the belief practice of selfless concern for the benefit of others.

Amino acid: amino acids are *molecules* that combine to form *proteins*. Amino acids and *proteins* are the building blocks of life. See Appendix B for additional discussion.

Anthropic universe: a universe that supports the existence of intelligent life.

Antiparticle: a subatomic particle with the same *mass* as a particle of ordinary matter but opposite electric charge and magnetic moment. A positively charged positron is the antiparticle of the negatively charged *electron*.

Atom: the smallest component of an *element*. Each atom has a *nucleus* containing positively charged *protons* and neutral *neutrons*. Negatively charged *electrons* orbit around the *nucleus* of the atom.

Autonomous: the quality or state of being independent, free, and self-directing.

Bacteria: a large group of single-cell microorganisms. Some cause infections and disease in animals and humans.

---

1. Terms in italics have their own entry in the glossary.

Glossary

Binary coding: a digital computer code in which there are only two possible states, off and on, usually designated by 0 and 1.

Biology: an area of science dealing with living organisms and their vital processes.

Biopolymer: a *polymer* occurring in living organisms Proteins and DNA are examples of biopolymers.

Black hole: a region in space having enormous *mass* packed into a tiny volume. The gravitational pull of a black hole is so strong that *light* cannot escape.

Blood clotting cascade: a series of chemical reactions that occurs during the formation of a blood clot.

Carnivore: an animal that feeds on flesh.

Catalyst: a substance which increases the rate of a chemical reaction without itself undergoing any permanent chemical change.

Cauda equina syndrome: occurs when the nerve roots in the lumbar spine are compressed, cutting off sensation and movement.

Celsius (°C): temperature scale in which water freezes at 0° and boils at 100°.

Chance: a possibility of something happening.

Chromosome: a structure found inside the *nucleus* of a cell. A chromosome is made up of *proteins* and DNA organized into *genes*. Each cell normally contains 23 pairs of chromosomes.

Clotting factor: a *protein* in blood that helps form blood clots to stop bleeding when an injury occurs.

CMB Cosmic *microwave* background *radiation*: CMB is a faint glow of *electromagnetic radiation* that fills the universe, and falls on Earth from every direction with nearly uniform intensity.

COBE Cosmic Background Explorer satellite: COBE took precise measurements of the diffuse *radiation* between 1 micrometer and 1 cm over the whole celestial sphere.

Glossary

Convergent evolution: the process by which different organisms that are not closely related independently evolve similar traits to adapt to necessities of survival.

Cosmic rays: high-energy particles or clusters of particles (primarily consisting of *protons* or atomic nuclei) that move through space at nearly the speed of *light*.

Cosmology: the science of the origin and development of the universe.

Creationism: the belief that the living organisms originate from acts of divine creation rather than by the natural process of evolution.

Design imperative: the requirement to optimally *design* subject to problem-solving constraints a component, system, or process that will perform a specified task subject to certain solution constraints.

Design: to construct or create or execute according to plan.

Deuterium: a stable *isotope* of *hydrogen* containing one *proton* and one *neutron* in its *nucleus*.

DNA: deoxyribonucleic acid, the hereditary material in humans and almost all other organisms. Nearly every cell in a person's body has the same DNA.

Doppler shift: the change in wave *frequency* when the wave source and observer move relative to one another. It was discovered by Christian Johann Doppler in 1842.

Electromagnetic force: the electromagnetic *force* is a type of physical interaction that occurs between electrically charged particles. The electromagnetic *force* is the combination of all magnetic and electrical *forces* between the particles. See Appendix A.

Electromagnetic radiation: *radiation* that has both electric and magnetic fields and travels in waves. It comes from natural and man-made sources. Electromagnetic *radiation* can vary in strength from low energy to high energy. It includes radio waves, *microwaves, infrared light, visible light, ultraviolet light,* x-rays, and gamma rays. See Appendix A.

Electron: a small negatively charged particle that is found in all *atoms*.

Glossary

Element: contains *protons, neutrons,* and *electrons*. All *atoms* of an element, including *isotopes*, have the same number of *protons* in their *nucleus*.

Energy density: amount of energy contained in a unit volume of space.

Enzyme: a biological *catalyst* that is almost always a *protein*. It speeds up the rate of a specific chemical reaction in the cell.

Ex nihilo: out of nothing (Latin).

Fahrenheit (°F): temperature scale in which water freezes at 32° and boils at 212°.

Feedback loop: a process where the outputs of a system are sent back and used to change inputs to the process.

Fibrin: a *protein* involved in forming *blood clots* in the body. It is made from the *protein fibrinogen* and helps stop bleeding and heal wounds.

Fibrinogen: a *protein* involved in forming *blood clots* in the body. It is made in the liver and forms *fibrin*

Fission: splitting or breaking *atoms* into parts.

Force: a push or a pull on an object in a particular direction.

Frequency: the number of times a wave moves past a fixed point per unit of time.

Fusion: combining or joining two or more atomic nuclei together to form a heavier *nucleus*.

Galaxy: a system of numerous stars (millions or billions), plus gas and dust, held together by gravitational attraction. Galaxies can be elliptical, irregular, peculiar, or spiral.

Gene duplication: a type of *mutation* that involves the production of one or more copies of a gene or region of a *chromosome*.

Gene: the basic physical and functional unit of heredity. Genes are made up of *DNA*. Some genes act as instructions to make *molecules* called *proteins*. However, many genes do not code for *proteins*. In humans, genes vary in size from a few hundred *DNA* bases to more than two million bases.

Glossary

Global optimum: an optimal solution where there are no other feasible solutions with better objective function values, i.e. the best possible solution.

Gravitational force: an attractive *force* that pulls objects with *mass* together.

Helium: a gas that has two *protons* in its *nucleus*. Helium exists in two stable *isotopes* which have one and two *neutrons* in their nuclei respectively.

Hemoglobin: a *protein* inside red blood cells that carries oxygen from the lungs to tissues and organs in the body and carries carbon dioxide back to the lungs.

Herbivore: an animal that feeds on plants.

Hominid: the group consisting of all modern and extinct Great Apes. The group includes modern humans, chimpanzees, gorillas and orang-utans plus all their immediate ancestors.

Homo sapiens: the primate species of primates which contains modern humans. Homo is Latin for "man" and sapiens Latin for "wise."

Hoyle state: an excited, resonant state of carbon. See discussion in chapter 3.

Hydrogen: a chemical *element* that is the lightest of all chemical *elements*. Hydrogen has one *proton* in its *nucleus*. Hydrogen is a colorless odorless highly flammable gas having two *atoms* per *molecule*.

Infrared: a region of *electromagnetic radiation* where *wavelengths* range from about 700 nanometers (*nm*) to 1 millimeter (*mm*). See Appendix A.

Intelligent design: the theory that life was designed and created by some intelligent entity, and evolution cannot explain all aspects of life.

Intergalactic: situated in or relating to the space between galaxies.

Irreducible complexity: a system with parts performing a basic function such that each part is indispensable to maintaining the system's basic function.

Isotope: *atoms* with the same number of *protons* in their nuclei, but different numbers of *neutrons*.

Glossary

Kelvin (°K): absolute temperature scale where water freezes at 273° and boils at 373°. Lowest possible temperature is absolute °K = 0.

Kilometer: a unit of measurement of length equal to 1,000 *meters* or 0.62 mile.

Left ventricle: one of four chambers of the heart.

Light: a form of energy. See Appendix A.

Light absorption: a process in which *light* is absorbed.

Light scattering: a process where a particle of *light* is absorbed by a substance and then emitted.

Magnetic field: the space around the magnet where its magnetic *force* can be felt.

Mass density: *mass* per unit volume.

Mass: the amount of matter contained in a particle or physical body.

Median nerve: the median nerve predominantly provides motor innervation to the flexor muscles of the forearm and hand as well as those muscles responsible for flexion, abduction, opposition, and extension of the thumb.

Metallicity: the proportion of the *mass* of a *star* that is *elements* other than *hydrogen* or *helium*.

Meteorite: a fragment of spatial material that hits the surface of a planet.

Meter: a unit of length equal to approximately 39.37 inches.

Microwave: an electromagnetic wave with a *wavelength* in the range 0.001–0.3 *meters*. See Appendix A.

Milky Way: a *galaxy* with a very large collection of stars, dust, and gas. Our Sun resides in the Milky Way.

Millimeter: a unit of length equal to one thousandth of a *meter*.

mm: see *millimeter*.

Model: a mathematical representation of a process.

Glossary

Molecule: molecules are made up of one or more *atoms*. If they contain more than one *atom*, the *atoms* can be the same (an oxygen molecule has two oxygen *atoms*) or different (a water molecule has two *hydrogen atoms* and one oxygen *atom*). Biological molecules, such as *proteins* and *DNA*, can be made up of many thousands of *atoms*.

Momentum: a measurement of *mass* in motion.

Multiverse: the proposal that beyond the observable universe, other universes exist as well. The multiverse cannot be observed.

Mutation: any change in the *DNA* sequence of a cell. Mutations may be caused by mistakes during cell division, or they may be caused by exposure to *DNA*-damaging agents in the environment.

Myocardium: the muscle tissue of the heart.

Nanometer: a unit of length equal to one billionth of a *meter*.

Neutron: an uncharged atomic particle that has a *mass* slightly larger than that of a *proton*.

nm: see *Nanometer*.

Nucleus: a positively charged region in the center of an *atom*. The nucleus consists of positively charged *protons* and neutral *neutrons* clustered together.

Objective: the goal of a *design imperative*.

Polymer: a class of natural or synthetic substances having a very large *molecules* which are multiples of simpler chemical units.

Probabilistic: based on how likely it is that something will happen.

Problem-solving constraints: involve what an engineering designer knows or is able to do.

Protein: a *polymer molecule* made up of amino acids.

Proton: a small, positively charged particle of matter.

Quantum computer: a computer that makes use of the *quantum* states of subatomic particles to store information. *Quantum* computers are more efficient than digital computers.

Glossary

Quantum indeterminacy: the assertion that the state of a system does not determine a unique collection of values for all its measurable properties.

Quantum: the smallest discrete unit of a phenomenon.

Radar: a device that uses radio *electromagnetic radiation* waves to detect and locate the speed and position an object by the reflection of the radio waves. See Appendix A.

Radiation: energy that comes from a source and travels through space at the speed of *light*. The energy has an electric field and a *magnetic field* associated with it, and has wave-like as well as particle-like properties. See Appendix A.

Radiocarbon: a type of carbon which is radioactive, and which very slowly undergoes *fission* to nitrogen.

Random: a sequence of events that has no order and does not follow an intelligible pattern. Random events cannot be predicted.

Redshift: the *wavelength* of the *light* is stretched, so the *light* is measured as shifted towards the longer *wavelength*, red part of the spectrum. See Appendix A.

Reinforcement: the action of strengthening something.

Serine protease: *enzymes* that cleave peptide bonds in *proteins*.

Siblicide: the killing of a sibling.

Solution constraints: in *design*, involve issues like the *design's* functionality, safety, reliability, and conformity to standards and legal codes.

Spectroscopy: the science of the absorption and emission of *light* and other *radiation* by matter.

Speed of light: in a vacuum, the speed of *light* is 186,000 miles per second.

Star: a massive celestial body of gas that radiates *light* derived from nuclear *fusion* taking place within it.

Strong nuclear force: one of four fundamental *forces* in nature. The strong nuclear *force* holds atomic nuclei together.

Glossary

Tectonics: a branch of geology dealing with the crust of a planet or Moon and particularly with the formation of folds and faults in it.

Thermostat feedback: a thermostat that controls the temperature by using a controller that increases or decreases the heat to a system based on its sensed temperature.

Thrombi: blood clots.

Tidal locking: the phenomenon by which a body has the same rotational period as its orbital period around a partner. Our Moon is tidally locked to the Earth and we see only one side of the moon.

Trephine opening: the removal of a disk of bone from the skull.

Tsunami: a series of large ocean waves of usually generated by a violent undersea disturbance.

Ultraviolet: *electromagnetic radiation* having a *wavelength* shorter than that of visible *light* but longer than that X-rays. See Appendix A.

Visible light: *electromagnetic radiation* with *wavelengths* between 380 and 750 *nanometers* which is visible to the human eye. See Appendix A.

Vitamin: a nutrient that the body needs in small amounts to function and stay healthy.

Wavelength: the distance between successive crests of a wave. See Appendix A.

X-ray scattering: scattering of X-rays by the *electrons* of an atomic shell.

Bibliography

Algren, Nathan. "What Is a Protein. A Biologist Explains." The Conversation, Jan 13, 2021. https://theconversation.com/what-is-a-protein-a-biologist-explains-152870#.[1]
Alpher, Ralph., and Robert Herman. "Evolution of the Universe." *Nature* 162 (1948) 774–75.
Anderson, Bianca. "AstroFan: Galaxy Types!" Adler Planetarium, Jan. 24, 2020. https://www.adlerplanetarium.org/blog/astrofan-galaxy-types/.
"Apostles Creed." US Conference of Catholic Bishops. https://www.usccb.org/prayers/apostles-creed.
Apostoli, Andrew. *Fátima For Today: The Urgent Maria Message of Hope.* San Francisco: Ignatius, 2010.
"Atom Formation in Stars." National Science Foundation. https://new.nsf.gov/science-matters/stars-within-us.
Barbour, Ian. *When Science Meets Religion.* New York: Harper Collins, 2000.
"Biochemistry." Britannica. https://www.britannica.com/science/Biochemistry.
Brockhaus, Hannah. "FULL TEXT: Benedict XVI shares his final thoughts with the Church." Catholic News Agency, Dec 31, 2022. https://www.catholicnewsagency.com/news/253202/full-text-of-benedict-xvis-spiritual-testament.
"Carbon Formation." Wikipedia. https://en.wikipedia.org/wiki/Carbon-12.
Caro, Liberato, et al. "X-ray Dating of a Turin Shroud's Linen Sample." *Heritage* 5 (2022) 860–70.
Carroll, Lewis. *Alice in Wonderland.* New York: Holt, Rhinehart, and Winston, 1923.
Casabianca, Tristan, et al. "Radiocarbon Dating of the Turin Shroud: New Evidence from Raw Data." *Archaeometry* 61 (2019) 1223–31.
"The Catholic Nicene Creed." Beginning Catholic. https://www.beginningcatholic.com/catholic-nicene-creed.
"Cells Can Replicate Their DNA Precisely." Scitable. https://www.nature.com/scitable/topicpage/cells-can-replicate-their-dna-precisely-6524830/.
"Chromosomes". National Human Genome Research Institute. https://www.genome.gov/about-genomics/fact-sheets/Chromosomes-Fact-Sheet.
"Convergent Evolution." Wikipedia. https://en.wikipedia.org/wiki/Convergent_evolution.

---

1. When inputting a link on a browser the period at the end should be eliminated, since with it in the link sometimes cannot be found.

Bibliography

Cook, Charles, el al. "B^{12}, C^{12}, and the Red Giants". *Physical Review* 107 (1957) 508.

"CMBR. Cosmic Microwave Background Radiation." Wikipedia. https://commons.wikimedia.org/wiki/File:Cmbr.svg.

"Cosmic Rays." Wikipedia. https://en.wikipedia.org/wiki/Cosmic_ray.

Coyne, Jerry. "The Case Against Intelligent Design." Edge, Nov 3 2023. https://www.edge.org/conversation/jerry_a_coyne-the-case-against-intelligent-design.

Crosswell, Ken. "'Goldilocks' Stars May Pose Challenges for Any Nearby Planets." Science News, April 20, 2022. https://www.sciencenews.org/article/orange-dwarf-stars-radiation-goldilocks-habitable-planets.

Damon, Paul., et al. "Radiocarbon Dating of the Shroud of Turin." *Nature* 337 (1989) 611–15.

Darwin, Charles. *On the Origin of Species*. London: John Murray, 1859.

Darwin, Charles. *The Descent of Man*. London: John Murray, 1871.

Davies, Paul. "A Brief History of the Multiverse." *The New York Times*, April 12, 2003. https://www.nytimes.com/2003/04/12/opinion/a-brief-history-of-the-multiverse.html.

Dawkins, Richard. *The Selfish Gene*. Oxford: Oxford University Press, 1976.

Dennett, Daniel. *Darwin's Dangerous Idea*. New York: Simon & Schuster, 1995.

"Department Position on Evolution and Intelligent Design." Lehigh University, Biological Sciences. https://www.lehigh.edu/~inbios/News/evolution.html.

Dicke, Robert. "Dirac's Cosmology and Mach's Principle." *Nature* 192 (1961) 440–41.

Domning, Daryl, and Monica Hellwig. *Original Selfishness: Original Sin and Evil in the Light of Evolution*. Burlington: Ashgate, 2006.

Doolittle, Russell. *The Evolution of Vertebrate Blood Clotting*. Sausalito: University Science, 2003.

"Double Slit Experiment." Wikipedia. https://commons.wikimedia.org/wiki/File:TwoSlit_Experiment_Light.svg.

"Earth's Magnetic Field." Wikipedia. https://commons.wikimedia.org/wiki/File:Earth%27s_magnetic_field,_schematic.png.

Edgar, Thomas, et al. *Optimization of Chemical Processes*. Second Edition. New York: McGraw Hill, 2001.

Einstein, Albert. *Ideas and Opinions*. New York: Citadel, 1956.

"Electromagnetic Spectrum." NASA. https://imagine.gsfc.nasa.gov/Images/science/EM_spectrum_compare_level1_lg.jpg.

"Electromagnetism." BYJU'S. https://byjus.com/physics/electromagnetism/.

"Eucharistic Miracles of Buenos Aires." Miracolieucaristici, 1992, 1996. http://www.miracolieucaristici.org/en/liste/scheda_c.html?nat=argentina&wh=buenosaires&ct=Buenos%20Aires,%201992–1994-1996.

"Eucharistic Miracle of Legnica." Miracolieucaristici, Dec 15, 2013. http://www.miracolieucaristici.org/en/download/legnica.pdf.

"Eucharistic Miracle of Sokolka." Real Presence, Oct 12, 2008. http://www.therealpresence.org/eucharst/mir/english_pdf/Sokolka1.pdf.

"Eucharistic Miracles of Tixla, 2006." St. Michael the Archangel Catholic Church, Oct 2006. https://www.stmike.org/from-the-pastors-desk/eucharistic-miracles-tixla-2006.

"Evolution." Merriam-Webster. https://www.merriam-webster.com/dictionary/evolution.

"Faith." Wikipedia. https://en.wikipedia.org/wiki/Faith.

Fanti, Giulio and Robert Siefker. *The Holy Fire and the Divine Photography*. Singapore: Jenny Stanford, 2023.

Bibliography

Fanti, Giulio, and Pierandrea Malfi. *The Shroud of Turin: First Century after Christ! Second Edition.* Singapore: Jenny Stanford, 2020.

Fanti, Giulio. "Holy Fire and Body Image of the Holy Shroud: Divine Photography Hypothesis." *World Scientific News* 176 (2023) 104–20.

Feynman, Richard. *The Character of Physical Law Variant.* London: Penguin, 1965.

"Fine Tuned Universe." HandWiki. https://handwiki.org/wiki/Astronomy:Fine-tuned_universe.

"Five Different Types of Spectroscopy." Platypus Technologies. https://www.platypustech.com/5-different-types-of-spectroscopy.

"Galapagos Finches." Darwin Online, 1845 Beagle F14 fig07.jpg. http://darwin-online.org.uk/converted/published/1845_Beagle_F14/.

"Gene." National Cancer Institute. https://www.cancer.gov/publications/dictionaries/genetics-dictionary/def/gene.

Glynn, Paul. *Healing Fire of Christ.* San Francisco: Ignatius, 2003.

"God the Geometer." Wikipedia. https://commons.wikimedia.org/wiki/File:God_the_Geometer.jpg.

Gould, Stephen. *Wonderful Life.* New York: Norton, 1989.

Gregersen, Erik. "Red Dwarf Star." Britannica. https://www.britannica.com/science/red-dwarf-star.

Guillen, Michael. *Believing Is Seeing.* Carol Stream, IL: Tyndale House, 2021.

Gunn, Alastair. "How Did Mars Lose Its Atmosphere." BBC Science Focus. https://www.sciencefocus.com/space/how-did-mars-lose-its-atmosphere/.

Haught, John. *Deeper Than Darwin.* Boulder: Westview, 2003.

Haught, John. *God After Darwin.* Boulder: Westview, 2008.

Heisenberg, Werner. "Ueber den anschaulichen Inhalt der quantentheoretischen Kinematik und Mechanik." *Zeitschrift für Physik.* 43 (1927) 172–98.

Henry, Richard, and Guy Worthey. "The Distribution of Heavy Elements in Spiral and Elliptical Galaxies." *Publications of the Astronomical Society of the Pacific* 111 (1999) 919–45.

Herbert, Nick. *Quantum Reality.* New York: Anchor, 1997.

"Hidden Life of Galaxies." NASA, Goddard Space Flight Center, May 7, 2015. https://imagine.gsfc.nasa.gov/educators/galaxies/imagine/hidden_mass.html.

Hoyle, Fred. "The Universe: Past and Present Reflections." *Engineering and Science* 45 (1981) 8–12.

Hubble, Edwin. "A Relation Between Distance and Radial Velocity among Extra-Galactic Nebulae." *Proceedings of National Academy of Sciences* 15 (1929) 168–73.

"Image of Our Lady of Guadalupe." Wikipedia. https://commons.wikimedia.org/wiki/File:Image_of_the_Virgin_Mary_at_the_new_Basilica_of_Our_Lady_of_Guadalupe,_Mexico_City.jpg.

"Intelligent Design." Wikipedia. https://en.wikipedia.org/wiki/Intelligent_design.

"Intelligent Design/Teleology." Intelligent Design Network. http://intelligentdesignnetwork.org/.

Kelly, Joseph. *The Problem of Evil in the Western Tradition. From the Book of Job to Modern Genetics.* Collegeville: Liturgical, 2002.

Kenneally, Christine. *The Invisible History of the Human Race: How DNA and History Shape Our Identities and Our Futures.* New York: Penguin, 2014.

Bibliography

Kowalski, Kyle. "Eternal Purpose: 'The Purpose Driven Life' by Rick Warren (Book Summary)." SLOWW. https://www.sloww.co/purpose-driven-life-book/#PDLmaster.

Kragh, Helge. "An Anthropic Myth: Fred Hoyle's Carbon-12 Resonance Level." *Archive for History of Exact Sciences* 64 (2010) 721–51.

"KT Event." NASA. https://www2.jpl.nasa.gov/sl9/back3.html.

Kuebler, Daniel. "Order, Chance and Design in Evolution." Purposeful Universe. https://www.purposefuluniverse.com/order-chance-and-design-in-evolution.

Kushner, Harold. *When Bad Things Happen to Good People*. New York: Avon, 1981.

Lanctot, Michael. "DOE Explains Nuclear Fusion Reactions." DOE Office of Science. https://www.energy.gov/science/doe-explainsnuclear-fusion-reactions.

Lederman, Leon, with Dick Teresi. *The God Particle*. Boston: Houghton Mifflin, 2006.

Lewis, Christopher. *Heat and Thermodynamics: A Historical Perspective*. Westport, CT: Greenwood, 2007.

"Lourdes. The Medical Bureau of the Sanctuary." Lourdes Sanctuaire. https://www.lourdes-france.org/en/medical-bureau-sanctuary/.

"Lourdes Medical Bureau-1." Wikipedia. http://en.wikipedia.org/wiki/Lourdes Medical Bureau.

"Lourdes Medical Bureau-2." Bionity. https://www.bionity.com/en/encyclopedia/Lourdes_Medical_Bureau.html.

MacDonald, John. "A Reducibly Complex Mousetrap." University of Delaware, Mar 14, 2011. https://udel.edu/~mcdonald/mousetrap.html.

Malthus, Thomas. *An Essay on the Principle of Population*. London: J. Johnson in St Paul's Church-yard, 1798.

Maxwell, James. *A Treatise on Electricity and Magnetism*. Cambridge: Cambridge University Press, 2010.

McLaughlin, Rebecca. *Confronting Christianity: 12 Hard Questions for the World's Largest Religion*. Wheaton: Crossway, 2019.

"Metabolic." National Cancer Institute. https://www.cancer.gov/publications/dictionaries/cancer-terms/def/metabolic#:~:text=(MEH%2Dtuh%2DBAH%2D,needed%20for%20important%20life%20processes).

Miller, Kenneth. *Finding Darwin's God*. New York: Harper Collins, 1999.

———"The Mousetrap Analogy, or Trapped by Design." millerandlevine.com. http://www.millerandlevine.com/km/evol/DI/Mousetrap.html.

"Miracle." Merriam-Webster. https://www.google.com/search?client=firefox-b-1-d&q=webster+miracle+definition.

"Miracles of Jesus." Wikipedia. https://en.wikipedia.org/wiki/Miracles_of_Jesus.

Mirsky, Steve. "Phrasing a Coyne: Jerry Coyne on Why Evolution Is True." *Scientific American*, Mar 13, 2009. https://www.scientificamerican.com/podcast/episode/phrasing-a-coyne-jerry-coyne-on-why-09-3-13/.

Monden, Louis. *Signs and Wonders. A Study of the Miraculous Element In Religion*. New York: Desclee, 1966.

Moriau, Bernadette. *My Life Is a Miracle*. Yonkers: Magnificat 2021.

Morris, Simon. *Life's Solution Inevitable Humans in a Lonely Universe*. Cambridge: Cambridge University Press, 2003.

"Mouse Trap." Wikipedia. https://commons.wikimedia.org/wiki/File:Lapki.jpg.

"Nagasaki after Atom Bomb." Wikipedia. https://upload.wikimedia.org/wikipedia/commons/c/cc/HD.4F.005_%2811873156176%29.jpg.

Bibliography

Newton, Isaac. *The Principia: The Authoritative Translation and Guide Mathematical Principles of Natural Philosophy*. Translated by I. Bernard Cohen et al. Oakland: University of California Press, 2016.

O'Connor, Patrick. "I Met a Miracle." Faith and Family. http://www.faithandfamily.org.uk/publications/jack_traynor.htm.

O'Connell Jerome, et al. "Pseudomyxoma peritonei is a disease of MUC2-expressing goblet cells." *American Journal of Pathology* 161 (2002) 551–64.

Oerter, Robert. *The Theory of Almost Everything*. New York: Pi, 2006.

"Original sin." Wikipedia. https://en.wikipedia.org/wiki/Original_sin.

"Our Lady of Guadalupe." Knights of Columbus. https://www.kofc.org/en/news-room/our-lady-of-guadalupe/the-story.html.

Pearl, Mike. "What the Nuclear Fusion Breakthrough Means for Our Future." Mashable, Dec. 13, 2022. https:// mashable.com/article/nuclear-fusion-ignition-breakthrough-lawrence-livermore.

Pfizenmaier, Thomas. "Was Isaac Newton an Alien?" *Journal of the History of Ideas* 58 (1997) 57–80.

"Photos from Vern Miller collection." Shroud Photos. https://shroudphotos.com/.

"Protein." Wikipedia. https://en.Wikipedia.org/wiki/Protein.

"Proteins Structure and Functions." BYJU'S. https://byjus.com/biology/proteins-structure-and-functions.

"Red Dwarf Stars." Wikipedia. https://en.wikipedia.org/wiki/Red_dwarf.

Rees, Martin. *Just Six Numbers*. New York: Basic Books, 2000.

Roser, Max, et al. "Life Expectancy." OurWorldInData, 2013. https://ourworldindata.org/life-expectancy.

Ruah, Judah. "Miracle of the Sun." *O Século*, Nov 9, 1917. https://commons.wikimedia.org/wiki/File:Miracle_of_the_Sun.jpg.

Ruse, Michael. *Can A Darwinian Be A Christian*. New York: Cambridge University Press, 2001.

Sagan, Carl. *Contact*. New York: Simon and Schuster, 1985.

"Science behind Our Lady of Guadalupe." Catholic News World. http://www.catholicnewsworld.com/2021/12/science-behind-our-lady-of-guadalupe-7.html.

"Science (or Lack Therof) behind Juan Diego's Tilma." Magis Center. https://www.magiscenter.com/blog/the-science-or-lack-thereof-behind-juan-diegos-tilma.

"Secrets of Her Image." Knights of Columbus. https://www.kofc.org/en/resources/cis/10575-secrets-of-her-image-poster.pdf.

"Shape and Structure of Proteins." National Library of Medicine. https://www.ncbi.nlm.nih.gov/books/NBK26830/.

Shigley, Joseph, et al. *Mechanical Engineering Design*. Seventh Edition. New York: McGraw Hill, 2004.

Siegel, Ethan. "The Strongest Evidence for a Universe before the Big Bang." Big Think, Mar 16, 2023. https://bigthink.com/starts-with-a-bang/evidence-universe-before-big-bang/.

———. "How Does the CMB Prove the Big Bang." Big Think, Sept. 30, 2022. https://bigthink.com/starts-with-a-bang/cmb-prove-big-bang/.

———. "Why is Fusion in Stars Different Than During the Big Bang." Big Think, May 12, 2022. https://bigthink.com/starts-with-a-bang/fusion-stars-big-bang/.

Bibliography

Silva, Lara. "What Happened at the Miracle of Fátima." Portugal.com, Dec 14, 2021. https://www.portugal.com/history-and-culture/what-happened-at-the-miracle-of-Fátima/.

Singh, Simon. *The Big Bang*. New York: Harper Collins, 2004.

Skarlakidis, Haris. *Holy Fire*. Athens: Elea, 2015.

"Solar System." Wikipedia. A.https://en.wikipedia.org/wiki/Historical_models_of_the_Solar_System#/media/File:Solar_system_scale-2.jpg; B. https://en.wikipedia.org/wiki/File:Solar-system.png

Spencer, Herbert. *Principles of Biology, Volume 1*. London: Williams and Norgate, 1864.

"Spiral Galaxy." Wikipedia. https://en.wikipedia.org/wiki/Spiral_galaxy#/media/File:M101_hires_STScI-PRC2006-10a.jpg.

Spitzer, Robert. *New Proofs for the Existence of God*. Grand Rapids: Wm. B. Eerdmans, 2010.

Strobel, Lee. *The Case For A Creator*. Grand Rapids: Zondervan, 2014.

"STURP: Shroud of Turin Research Project." Wikipedia. https://en.wikipedia.org/wiki/Shroud_of_Turin_Research_Project.

"Survival of Fittest." Wikipedia. https://en.wikipedia.org/wiki/Survival_of_the fittest.

Thaxton, Charles. *Of Pandas and People*. Mesquite: Haughton, 1989.

"Types of Stars." Las Cumbres Observatory, Goleta. https://lco.global/spacebook/stars/types-stars/.

"Uses of Electromagnet." BYJU'S. https://byjus.com/physics/uses-of-electromagnet.

van Haelst, Remi. "Radiocarbon Dating the Shroud: a Critical Statistical Analysis." https://www.shroud.com/vanhels3.htm.

"Visible Lives of Galaxies." NASA, Goddard Space Flight Center, May 7, 2015. https://imagine.gsfc.nasa.gov/educators/galaxies/imagine/characteristics.html.

Ward, Peter, and Donald Brownlee. *Rare Earth: Why Complex Life Is Uncommon in the Universe*. New York: Copernicus, 2004.

Warren, Rick. *The Purpose Driven Life*. Grand Rapids: Zondervan, 2002.

"What Is DNA." National Library of Medicine. https://medlineplus.gov/genetics/understanding/basics/dna/.

"What Is Radiation." Centers for Disease Control. https://www.cdc.gov/nceh/radiation/what_is.html.

"What Is the Shroud of Turin." Catholic Straight Answers. https://catholicstraightanswers.com/what-is-the-shroud-of-turin/.

"What Is Weather Radar." IBM. https://www.ibm.com/weather/industries/broadcast-media/what-is-weather-radar.

Whitaker, Bill. "France's Sanctuary of Our Lady of Lourdes." CBS News 60 Minutes, Dec 18 2022. https://www.cbsnews.com/news/sanctuary-of-our-lady-of-lourdes-miracles-cures-2022-12-18/.

Williams, Jeanette. "The Amazing Science of Recent Eucharistic Miracles: A Message from Heaven." Ascension Press, Nov 3, 2021. https://media.ascensionpress.com/2021/11/03/the-amazing-science-of-recent-eucharistic-miracles-a-message-from-heaven/.

Xu, Xun, and Russell Doolittle. "Presence of a Vertebrate Fibrinogen-like Sequence in an Echinoderm." *Proceedings of the National Academy of Sciences* 87 (1990) 2097–101.

Zimmer, Carl. *Evolution the Triumph of an Idea*. New York: Harper Collins, 2001.

Index

alanine, 135–36
algorithm, 56–61, 137–41, 143
   characteristics, 56
   definition, 56
   genetic, 58, 137–41
   purpose, 58
   steepest ascent, 141
Alpher, Ralph, 17, 20–21
altruism
   biological, 63
   moral, 63
   true, 63–64, 66–67, 125–26
amino acid, 134–36, 143, 149
antiparticle, 78, 143
Apostoli, Andrew, 11, 96, 105, 118–19
apparition, 113, 115, 118–19
astronomy, 6
atmosphere, 42, 133
   orbiting planet's, 40–41
atom
   built from fusion, 25, 28
   definition, 143
   destroyed by fission, 25
   energy required for production, 24–25
   heavier, 22, 28
   location, 5
   spectral radiation, 77
   strong nuclear force, 27–28
bases, 50, 83, 146
Behe, Michael, 69–73, 75
Big Bang, 12–25
   carbon formation, 22, 29

cosmic microwave background radiation (CMB), 20, 23, 26, 144
   energy implications, 16, 24–25, 122
   expansion, 17
   fine-tuning, 23, 26–46, 67, 123
   first few minutes, 2, 15–16, 18–20, 132
   fusion reactions, 19
   hydrogen helium ratio, 20
   inflation, 15
   prior to, 124
   star formation after, 21
   temperature, 13
   theory, 12, 17, 21–23, 26
binary coding, 139, 144
black hole, 14, 37, 144
blood, 101, 144
   clotting, 69, 72–74, 144, 146
   clotting factors, 72–73, 144
   Eucharistic miracles, 117
   Shroud of Turin, 107
brancardier, 101–4
Brownlee, Donald, 35–36, 38, 41, 43, 45
candle, 110–12
carbon, 17, 20, 22, 28–29, 38, 74, 135–36, 147
   abundance, 30
   dioxide, 42, 147
   radioactive, 150
   resonance state of, 22, 29–30
   theory of formation, 22
carnivorous, 88
Casabianca, Tristan, 109, 153

Index

cell, 35, 49–50, 53, 72, 86, 131, 134, 144–46, 149
chance, 84–85
   creation of universe, 45
   definition, 144
   events, 52, 70, 84–86
   role in evolution, 51–52, 54–55, 67, 96, 123
charged particle, 20, 130, 132, 145, 149
Christ, 65–66, 106, 108, 124
Christian, 4, 65–66, 97, 119
Christianity, 66, 112
   evolution, 4, 66
   Light, 80–81
   original sin, 124
chromosome, 49, 146
   definition, 144
CMB. *See* Big Bang, cosmic microwave background radiation
Committee of Lourdes (CMIL), 98
conflict
   between faith and science, 1, 4, 11, 66
   model, 5–6
   original sin, 125
constant
   cosmological, 14
   narrow range, 23, 27–29, 31
   physical, 26, 31–33, 45, 67
continental drift, 41
Copernicus, 3, 158
cosmic rays, 145
   Earth's atmosphere, 131
   origin, 42
Coyne, Jerry, 69, 74, 156
creation, 9–10, 30, 34, 45, 66, 127
   Big Bang, 15
   energy involved, 25
   ex nihilo, 23
   intelligence behind, 32, 34, 45
   natural evil, 91
   stories, 12, 47, 88–89, 124
creationism, 68–69
creation science, 69, 124
Creator, 7, 10, 35, 56, 82–83, 86, 93, 122
creature, 54–55, 82–83
cure, 96–99, 104–5
   by Jesus, 96
   John Traynor, 97, 99, 104–5
   Lourdes, 97–99, 105
   medically inexplicable, 98

Darwin, Charles, 4, 47–48, 51, 59, 63, 141
Dawkins, Richard, 61–62, 64, 125
Dennett, Daniel, 47, 52, 56–58, 64, 67
density, 19, 31
design, 70, 91, 145, 150
   automobile, 8
   autonomous, 9–10, 91, 122–23
   engineering, 7–8, 121
   in evolution, 52
   goal, 46
   imperative, 8–10, 23–25, 33–34, 46, 55, 67, 76, 86, 90, 94, 120–23
   mousetrap, 71
   objective, 9, 122
   solution constraints, 9–10
   universe, 7–9, 55, 83, 93–94, 121–22
Designer, 7, 10, 93
dialog
   between faith and science, 6
   model, 5–6
Diego, Juan, 112–15
dinosaur, 52–54
direction, 141, 144
   Big Bang, 56
   cosmological constant, 14
   of evolution, 10, 48, 56, 61
   magnetic field, 28
   of nature, 85
   toward altruism, 64, 126
   toward suffering, 126
disorder, 95–96, 98
distance, 14–15, 35–36, 38, 40, 133, 151
DNA, 144–46, 149
   coding errors, 51, 83, 149
   definition, 49, 145
   information storage, 50
   radiation, 131
doctors, 101–4, 113, 117
Domning, Daryl, 125
Doolittle, Russell, 73–74
double slit experiment, 78–80
dust, 86, 89, 146, 148

Index

Earth
    axis of rotation, 43–44
    evolution, 4, 10, 35, 51, 61, 76
    existence, 9
    galactic orbit, 38
    interior fission reactions, 42
    Jupiter, 43–45, 53
    magnetic field, 42, 130–31, 154
    Moon, 43, 151
    natural evil, 87, 89
    plate tectonics, 41, 91
    size, 36
    stardust, 22
    surface, 90–91
    temperature, 42, 44, 90
earthquake, 85, 87, 90
Eden, 88–89, 91, 124
Edicule, 110, 112
Einstein, Albert, 4, 13–14, 17, 82
electromagnetic
    force, 11, 19, 21, 28–29, 129–30, 145
    radiation, 4, 131–32, 144–45, 147, 150–51
    waves, 20, 131–33, 148
electromagnetism, 4, 29, 129–30
electron, 17, 19–20, 28–29, 77–78, 81–83, 131, 143, 145–46, 151
electron volts, 30
element, 17, 19, 38, 143, 146–48
energy
    atomic fission explosions, 24
    atomic fusion, 18
    atomic fusion in Sun, 19
    Big Bang, 13, 24, 122
    conversion to mass, 17
    density, 146
    electron volt, 30
    light, 148
    radiation, 78, 110, 131–32, 148, 150
    red dwarf stars, 40
enzyme, 46, 72–73, 146, 150
    cascade, 72–73
eternal life, 65–67
evidence
    against irreducible complexity, 72
    Big Bang, 15
    Eucharistic miracles, 116–17
    evolution, 10, 48, 74
    John Traynor, 105
    Our Lady Guadalupe, 113
    physical miracle, 76, 96–97, 104, 118
evil, 85, 87, 89, 91, 94, 122
    moral, 87, 89–90
    natural, 55, 84, 87–91, 93–94, 123
evolution
    algorithm, 56, 58, 60–61, 138, 140–41
    biological, 52, 60, 123, 139–40
    chance, 52, 67, 70, 96, 123
    change, 51, 61, 93
    conflict, 63
    conflict with faith, 4, 66–67
    continuous slow, 4, 25, 34
    convergent, 53, 145, 153
    cooperation, 62–63, 125
    definition, 47
    direction, 10, 56, 70, 76
    human, 4, 9, 130
    mutation, 51, 93
    order, 52–53, 55, 67
    process, 10, 25, 34, 48, 51, 53–54, 56, 61–62, 64, 75, 125
    purpose, 48, 52, 56–67, 70
    rerun, 47, 51–55, 67
    theory, 47–48, 51, 68, 137
existence, 41, 52–53
    Earth-like planets, 38
    free will, 84
    God, 7, 96, 105, 122–23
    other universes, 32, 127
    soul, 85
experts, 65–66, 104, 117

facts
    physical, 5–6, 120
    scientific, 7, 35, 55, 108, 115
faith, 90, 93, 99, 112
    afterlife, 86
    Big Bang, 12, 105
    derivation of word, 3
    evolution, 7, 47, 51, 66–67
    miracles, 96–97, 105
    multiverse, 32–34
    and science, 1, 3–6, 11, 47, 118, 123–27
    today, 3
Fanti, Giulio, 109–12

Index

finch, 59–60
fission, 25, 78, 83, 146
fittest, 60–62, 64
flight, 53
force, 23, 28–29, 129–30, 132, 145–48, 150
fusion, 18–19, 21, 25, 28–29, 146

galaxy, 14, 25, 31, 36–38, 42, 146–48
   elliptical, 36, 38, 146
   irregular, 38
   spiral, 36–38, 146
Galileo, Galilei, 3–4
gamma ray, 131–32, 145
gene, 46, 51, 64–65, 73–75, 125, 139–40, 144, 146
   duplication, 73, 146
Genesis, 12, 23, 47, 88, 90, 124
genetic algorithms, 11, 58–60, 137–41
global optimum, 58–61, 141, 147
glycine, 135–36
Glynn, Paul, 97
Gould, Stephen, 47, 51, 67
grace, 51, 84–85, 92, 94–95
gravity, 13–14, 21–22, 29, 31
   force, 21, 28, 37, 43–44, 129, 144, 147
Grotto of Lourdes, 98, 101–3
Guadalupe, 106, 112, 114–15, 120
Guillen, Michael, 5, 80–81

Haught, John, 123
heaven, 12, 23, 116, 118
helium, 19–22, 27–28, 35, 38–39, 147–48
   atom, 20, 26–27
   nuclei, 18–19
Hellwig, Monica, 125
Holy Fire, 111–12
hominid, 62, 147
Homo sapiens, 9, 51, 55, 61–62, 147
Host, consecrated, 116–17
Hoyle, Fred, 22, 29–30, 32
Hoyle state, 29–30, 147
Hubble, Edwin, 14–15
human
   freedom, 10, 55, 82, 85–86, 90, 92, 94, 105, 120, 122
   modern, 62, 147
   nature, 66, 93–94
   survivability, 61
hydrogen, 16–17, 19–22, 28, 38, 135, 145, 147–48
   atom, 18, 20, 26, 135–36, 149
hydrogen and helium, 21–22

independence, model, 5–6
independent variable, 58
inflation, space, 15
information, 149
   genetic, 2, 49–50
   local, 59–60, 138, 140–41
integration, model, 5–6
Intelligent Design (ID), 7, 10, 48, 68–71, 73–76, 147
Intelligent Design Network, 69–70
intervention, 10, 76, 90, 105
irreducible complexity, 70, 72–75, 147
isotope, 16–17, 145–47

Jesus, 65–66, 92, 110, 117
   Light, 80–81
   miracles, 96
Jupiter, 35, 43–45, 53

Kenneally, Christine, 126
KT event, 45, 52–54
Kuebler, Daniel, 52–55
Kushner, Harold, 88, 93–94

latitude, 138–40
laws of nature, 93–94
length, 5, 82, 148–49
life, 85–86, 88–89
   complex, 36, 38, 40–43, 45
   on Earth, 2, 22–23, 26, 29, 31–32, 38, 40–45, 54–55, 91
   everlasting, 65, 67, 91
   evolution, 7, 10, 34–35, 41, 48, 61, 83, 93
   intelligent, 7, 9–10, 26–27, 45–47, 49, 51, 53–54, 56, 61, 67, 122
   nuclear fusion, 19
   on other planets, 36, 39–40
   primitive, 36, 45
   purpose, 52, 64, 92, 94
   support, 30, 32, 41

Index

light, 14, 37, 77, 79, 132, 148
   absorption, 109, 148
   and God, 80–81
   scattering, 109, 148
   speed, 17, 42, 80, 131, 150
local optima, 59, 141
longitude, 138–40
Lourdes, 97–105, 156, 158

magnet, 28–29, 130, 148
magnetic field, 11, 28, 42, 130–32, 145, 148, 150
Mars, 35, 42–44
mass, 17–20, 22, 24, 28, 31, 36, 39, 99, 143–44, 147–49
   density, 19, 21, 31, 148
mathematics, 5, 14
matter, 6, 13, 15, 37, 78, 80–83, 148–50
Medical Bureau of Lourdes, 97–98, 104
microwave, 11, 132, 148
Milky Way, 14, 37–38, 148
Miller, Kenneth, 51, 55, 71–72, 74, 77, 82
miracle, 123
   "data" for God's existence, 96
   definition, 95
   difference from ID, 76
   Fátima, 118–20
   healing, 95–105
   Holy Fire, 111
   Jesus, 96–97
   modern, 97
   modern Eucharistic, 116–17
   Our Lady Guadalupe, 114
   physical facts, 6, 10, 76, 96, 99, 106, 120
   rare, 10, 85, 96
   Shroud of Turin, 110
molecule, 72, 74, 77, 135, 143, 146–47, 149
momentum, 81–82, 149
Monden, Louis, 95–96
Moon, 35, 43–44, 54, 115, 151
Moriau, Bernadette, 98–99
Morris, Simon, 53
mousetrap, 71
multiverse, 32–33, 149
mutation, 51, 53, 55, 61, 83, 93, 146, 149
   genetic algorithm, 139–41

survivability, 51

NASA, 20, 26, 37–38
natural selection, 7, 54, 61, 63–64, 69, 71, 137
   survivability, 61
neutral atom, 19–21
neutron, 17–18, 27, 78, 143, 145–47, 149
next life, 86, 91–92
nitrogen, 17, 135–36, 150
non-believing scientist, 31–32, 47
non-scientist, 6–7, 11–12, 27, 47, 77
nucleus, 17–19, 27–28, 49, 143–47, 149

objective, 8–9, 91, 121–22
observer, 80, 133
O'Conner, Patrick, 99
offspring, 48–49, 54, 63–64, 137, 139–41
orbit, 17, 37–38, 143
   solar system's galactic, 37–38
organism, 48–50, 53, 83, 134, 137, 145
original sin, 124–27
Our Lady of Guadalupe, 106, 112, 114–15, 157
oxygen, 17, 20, 22, 28, 38, 117, 135–36, 147, 149

parent, 49, 88, 125, 137–41
particle, 5, 16–17, 19, 78–81, 130, 143, 145, 148
   subatomic, 16–17, 78, 81, 143, 149
peak, 58–59, 61, 138, 140–41
peptide bond, 136
physicist, 5, 16, 26, 78, 81
physics, 10, 16, 30, 77
planet, 45–46
   formation, 22
   habitable zone, 40
   orbiting orange dwarf stars, 41
   orbiting red dwarf stars, 39–40
   tidally locked, 40
plasma, 111
PMP, 87–89, 93
positron, 19, 78
probability, 45, 52, 78, 81, 84, 125
problem-solving constraints, 8–9, 121, 145, 149

Index

protein, 11, 46, 49–50, 72–74, 134–35, 143–44, 146–47, 149–50
    folding, 53, 136
proton, 18–19, 27–29, 42, 78, 81, 143, 145–47, 149
pseudoscience, 69, 75
purposeless, 10, 48, 56, 58

quantum
    event, 83
    indeterminacy, 77–86, 93, 96, 122, 150
    mechanics, 77, 80–82

radiation, 13, 19–20, 37–38, 110, 129, 132–33
    definition, 145
    mutations, 51, 131
radiocarbon dating, 108–9
reaction
    chemical, 42, 72, 84, 134, 144, 146
    nuclear, 18–19
Rees, Martin, 16, 23, 31–32
relativity, 13–14
religion, 4, 65–67, 69, 118
rosary, 11, 118–19
rotation, 43–44, 130
Ruse, Michael, 63, 93

science
    faith, 3–6, 10–11, 47, 123–27
    faith model, 5
    miracles, 6, 96
    modern, 1, 123
    Shroud of Turin, 110
scientific knowledge, 6, 17, 55, 76, 108
scientist, 1
    God creating universe, 32
    miracles, 6, 96
    religious beliefs, 4
    Shroud of Turin, 106
selfish behavior, 125–26
Shroud of Turin, 11, 106–10, 112, 114, 120
Shroud of Turin Research Project (STURP), 107–8
Siegel, Ethan, 15, 18–20
Singh, Simon, 12–14, 17, 22–24, 77

solar system, 25, 29, 34–39, 41–46, 66–67, 123, 132, 158
solution constraint, 8–10, 91, 94, 121–22, 145, 150
soul, 4, 55, 65, 86
space, 6, 23, 42
spectroscopy, 11, 132, 150, 155
Spitzer, Robert, 27–29, 31, 33
star
    atom production, 22, 28
    burn, 25, 39, 51
    definition, 150
    distance to, 14–15
    early, 21–22
    first, 21
    galaxies, 36–38
    habitable zone, 40
    metallicity, 38
    nuclear fusion, 21, 28
    red dwarf, 29, 39–41
    types, 39
    velocity relative to Earth, 14–15
statistical analysis, 108–9
Steady State theory, 22, 26
steepest ascent, 141
Strobel, Lee, 70, 72
strong nuclear force, 27–28, 129, 150
Sun
    cosmic rays, 42
    death, 22
    formation, 25
    metallicity, 38
    miracle at Fátima, 119
    solar system, 35–36
    type, 39, 41
survival, 49, 54–55, 60, 62, 64–65, 125, 140, 145
survival machine, 64

tectonic plate motion, 41–42, 90–91
temperature, 2, 13, 15, 19–21, 42, 112, 151
Tepeyac hill, 113–14
theologian, 90, 123, 125
theology, 12, 27, 89–90, 123
thorns, 85, 89, 91–92
thumbs, 108, 148
tidal locking, 40, 151

Index

tilma, 113–15, 120
time scale, 9–10, 25
tradeoff, 7–9, 91–94, 121, 123
trait, 49, 51, 54, 140, 145
trap, 42
Traynor, John, 97, 99–105
tsunami, 90, 151

universe
    anthropic, 26–28, 143
    beginning, 13, 15, 31, 33, 124
    best, 10, 90
    Big Bang, 9, 12–13, 16–17, 23, 31
    bouncing, 33–34
    creation, 12, 15–16, 30, 32, 34, 45, 56, 82, 124, 127
    dark energy, matter, 6
    design, 7–8, 10, 55, 67, 90–91, 93–94, 120–23
    early, 13, 28, 132
    eternal, 13, 33
    evolution, 9, 153
    expansion, 13–15, 19–21, 31

fine-tuning, 23, 26–27, 29, 31, 33–34, 45, 67, 123
freedom, 9, 83
hydrogen helium ratio, 20, 26
multiverse, 32–33, 149
star formation, 2

values, 23, 30–32, 138, 150
velocity, 81, 122
vertebrate, 73–74
Virgin, 113–15
vitamin, 74–75, 151
Volkov, Andrei, 110–11

Ward, Peter, 35–36, 38, 41–45
Warren, Rick, 84
water, 13, 31, 79, 91, 96–98, 101, 116–17, 135–36
wave, 79–81, 145–46, 150–51
    radio, 132, 145, 150
wavelength, 147–48, 150–51

x-ray, 11, 131–33, 145, 151

www.ingramcontent.com/pod-product-compliance
Lightning Source LLC
Chambersburg PA
CBHW072135160426
43197CB00012B/2112